Wallace-Homestead
PRICE GUIDE TO
AMERICAN COUNTRY
Antiques
15th EDITION

DON & CAROL RAYCRAFT

Published by

700 E. State Street • Iola, WI 54990-0001
Telephone: 715/445-2214

Please call or write for our free catalog. Our toll-free number to place an order or obtain a
free catalog is 800-258-0929 or please use our regular business telephone 715-445-2214
for editorial comment and further information.

Library of Congress Number: 86-6400023
ISBN: 0-87069-721-8
Printed in the United States of America

Cover photograph by Carol Raycroft
Photography by Don & Carol Raycroft

CONTENTS

Chapter 7—Advertising

Chapter 8—Shops, Markets and Auction Houses

Chapter 9—The Test

ACKNOWLEDGMENTS

A project of this magnitude requires a great deal of communication and cooperation. Without the assistance of the individuals and businesses listed below, it could not be completed. We sincerely appreciate their help and friendship.

American Harvest Antiques

American Roots

Aston Americana

Wilma Becker

Sharon Clymer

Don and Joyce Coffman

Collectors' Choice Antique Gallery

John Colteaux

Teri and Joe Dziadul

Michael L. Fallon

Ron Hall and Howard R. Hall

Todd and Marlene Harting

Stan Hollenbaugh

Lisha Holt

Dr. Alex Hood

Raymond Gerdes

Bernie Green

A. Gridley Antiques

Dick Harting

Brenda Jones

Joy and Robert Luke

Tony Macek

Thomas O'Donnell

Opal Pickens

R.C. Raycraft

Mike & Emily Raycraft

Ann Roop

Steve and Jetsy Sachtleben

John Stewart

DeeLores Teeters

Vicki and Bruce Waasdorp

Rick and Vanessa Wayne

Manuela Yokota

INTRODUCTION

The first generation of Americana collectors in the United States dates from little more than a century ago. Many of these individuals were more interested in "artifacts" that had come into contact with illustrious and historically important Americans than furnishing their homes.

From the 1940s through the 1960s, it did not take deep pockets or a great deal of knowledge to buy American country furniture because there was minimal competition from other collectors and a microscopic number of pieces that had newly painted surfaces or major cosmetic reworking.

Today, buying American country antiques of all kinds requires elastic pockets, a background check on the character of the individual offering the piece for sale, a paint-chip analysis, evaluation by a structural engineer, supreme confidence in your experience and ability to make rational decisions and an additional zero or two on the check.

The day after tomorrow, we will have the fourth or fifth generation of the original collectors searching abandoned grocery and discount stores that have been retrofitted as "antiques malls" for "rare" Pez dispensers and galvanized watering cans that will still be available for half the price at the Ace Hardware Store across the street.

CHAPTER 1

PRICE GUIDES, TRENDS & PREDICTIONS

Price Guides

We have once again contacted dealers and collectors across the United States to secure some insights into the current pricing structure, buying trends, attitudes and availability of a wide cross-section of country Americana. Unlike the price of silver or a Big Mac, which differ little from Cheyene to Sheyboygan, the real value of a pie safe or decorated stoneware crock is most often determined by the motivation of the buyer and the seller to reach an agreement.

A secondary factor may be where the transaction takes place. Obviously, there can be a significant difference in the asking price of a painted cupboard on the back porch of a home in Grey Lake, Ark., and a similar example at a prestigious Americana show in New York City.

The primary purpose of this price guide, from the authors' perspective, is to give collectors a general overview of the current marketplace for Americana and information about the direction it may be taking.

Trends

What's Hot	**What's Not**
Painted furniture	Photo opportunities with O.J. Simpson
Garden-related antiques	Fabio and Fabian
Lobster sandwich at Red's Eats, Wiscasset, Maine	A lunch of sausage gravy, biscuits and a strawberry milk shake
Advertising	Andy Warhol's cookie jars
Rustic furniture	Baseball cards issued ater 1970
Architectural antiques	Refinished pine furniture
Halloween-related collectibles from the 1920s-1950s	Commemorative plates
Buying trips to Illinois, Iowa and Indiana	Buying trips to South Dakota
Krispy Kremes	Galvanized watering cans
Nutmeg graters	Six Million Dollar Man lunch boxes
19th and early 20th century baseball memorabilia	Mediocre Shaker
Upscale Americana shows and a tailgate within walking distance	Goat carts from eastern Europe

Predictions

1. At an isolated antiques mall in an abandoned grocery store somewhere in Middle America, a curious customer will venture into a booth to check the price on an early Kibbles & Bits dog food package, trip over a pile of collectible wash rags and disappear.

2. Examples of country furniture and "smalls" that are classified by today's standards as mediocre and bring marginal dollars at auctions or rest forever in a dealer's booth or shop, eventually are going to become desirable, as upper end pieces disappear into collections (until death or divorce releases them again).

3. Look for a gradual rebound in the prices of midwestern quilts and coverlets. Stone fruit is also going to become more popular among mainstream collectors

Collecting Collectibles

The February 1997 issue of *House & Garden* magazine, in a short article, pointed out that many trendy New Yorkers are accessorizing their homes, apartments and lofts with sporting collectibles. These items include wooden tennis rackets, baseball gloves, lacrosse sticks, polo mallets and trophies. These collectibles are collected because "they evoke a more genteel time. They're very Gatsby."

A shopkeeper who sells sporting collectibles made an insightful comment by noting "There are new collectibles being invented every moment."

If you are going to become involved today in accumulating collectibles for your granddaughter's garage sale 30 years down the road, there are some basic rules you need to memorize:

1. You are leaving a mess rather than a legacy.

2. The law of diminishing marginal utility will still be valid on the day of the garage sale and two Tickle Me Elmos will bring the same amount of money and take up less space than nine Tickle Me Elmos.

3. You can add a codicil to your will that allows your collectibles to be buried with you. This will undoubtedly make your heirs and the local landfill operator especially glad.

CHAPTER 2

INVENTORY

The Complete Collector Inventory

If you are a serious collector of Americana, this list should outline many of the experiences you have already encountered along the pathway to claiming the title. Read the list, respond, add up your points and (possibly) rejoice in the moment. (Don't forget to deduct the minuses from your final total.)

You have a chronic fear of automatic car washes (2 points)   ——

You were in the sixth grade with someone named Skip, Chip or Junior (2 points)   ——

You have been alone in a hotel room with Bill
    Clinton and an Arkansas State Trooper (6 points)   ——

You sat behind Eva Braun in a high school German class (12 points)   ——

You once subscribed to *Country Living* (1 point)   ——

You had a summer job at the Texas School Book Depository in Dallas (3 points)   ——

You know who Robert Zimmerman of Hibbing, Minn., is (2 points)   ——

You know James Earl Ray and your nickname is Raul (5 points)   ——

You would have a lemonade shake-up rather than a glass of vintage red wine (3 points)   ——

You attended the world premiere of "Birth of a Nation" (8 points)   ——

You double dated to the prom with Mary Earle Gould in Worcester, Mass. (4 points)   ——

You have visited the following antiques venues in your collecting career:

    New Hampshire Dealers' Show (2 points)   ——
    Heart of Country in Nashville (2 points)   ——
    Towanda, Ill. July 4th Flea Market (5 points)   ——

You have had a lobster sandwich at Red's Eats in Wiscasset, Maine (3 points)   ——

You have given birth (2 points)   ——

You have attended antiques shows in California and
    Maine in the same calendar year (3 points)   ——

You have driven 300 miles to an antiques show and not bought anything (2 points)   ——

You own the previous 14 editions of this book (4 points)   ——

You have had hash browns for breakfast at a Waffle House (2 points)   ——

You sat through "Field of Dreams" without crying (2 points)   ——

You sat through "Old Yeller" without crying (2 points)   ——

You sat through "Strip Tease" with Demi Moore without leaving the theater (3 points)   ——

You would rather buy things than eat stuff (2 points)   ——

You own several pieces of carnival glass (-4 points)   ——

You eat dinner off of a round oak table with claw feet (-3 points)   ——

You have seen Ted Williams in person (3 points)   ——

You have taken a swim with Esther Williams (4 points)   ——

You can tie a bow tie (1 point)   —

You have received a speeding ticket on the way to an antiques show (2 points)   —

You would rather have a wisdom tooth pulled with a pair of pliers
    than take a country line-dancing lesson (1 point)   —

You are a subscriber to the *Maine Antiques Digest* (2 points)   —

You are a subscriber to *Carnival Glass Quarterly* (-4 points)   —

You were a prisoner during the Spanish-American War (12 points)   —

You got drunk at your last high school class reunion and have been
    permanently expunged from the Alumni Projectionists' Club (4 points)   —

You know what FFA stands for (2 points)   —

You can tell a Monet from mayonnaise (1 point)   —

You were caught sneaking into an antiques show or market before it opened (4 points)   —

You know the name of Little Lulu's boyfriend (2 points)   —

You have seen a movie star at an antiques show (3 points)   —

You purchased, at some point in your antiques career, a "bird" decorated
    stoneware jug or crock for $50 or less (5 points)   —

You paid more than $1,000 for a piece of stoneware (2 points)   —

You have been to the opera and eaten a hot dog "dressed" in the same day (3 points)   —

You have attended the outdoor antiques show in Dorset, Vt. (2 points)   —

You have been to an "antiques" show at a shopping mall in Peoria, Ill. (-2 points)   —

You have been to more than one "antiques" show at a shopping mall in Peoria, Ill. (-6 points)   —

You have purchased a baseball cap in Cooperstown, N.Y. (4 points)   —

You have paid at least $50 for "early bird" admission to an
    antiques show or market (4 points)   —

You can honestly say that Steve McQueen is your all-time favorite
    American movie star (4 points)   —

You have taken something out of a dumpster and put it in your home (1 point)   —

You have slept in a dumpster (3 points)   —

You bought something of consequence for your collection in North Dakota (3 points)   —

You have seen the following movies: (3 points for each complete group)

    a. "High Noon," "Goodfellas," "Casino," "Used Cars"   —
    b. "Citizen Kane," "The Godfather," "The Long Riders"   —
    c. "The Searchers," "Incident at Kickapoo Creek," "The Hollywood Knights"   —

Scoring

Over 130 points: Your score indicates that you are approaching antiques self-actualization and perpetual nirvana, but it probably won't happen.

100-129 points: You could be a self-confident guest authority at a noon Kiwanis meeting and receive a four-minute telephone card. Don't take any questions and leave before the Pledge of Allegiance.

75-99 points: You are capable of writing a collectibles column for any weekly paper in Idaho.

CHAPTER 3

ANTIQUES 103

Antiques 103

One of the early lessons that collectors must accept and digest is that the point in time when you make your appearance at an antiques show or market is highly correlated with your potential to find:

1. Something great that is under-priced.

2. Something great that is overpriced, but, nevertheless, is still great.

3. Absolutely nothing and save your-self the rest of the day.

4. Merchandise for potential resale with semi-significant dollars left for profit.

5. An item that is "good" and located in the booth of a dealer who handles a different type of merchandise that normally you would skip in your trip through the crowded show.

6. The time to leisurely examine a piece of furniture and talk to the sell-er without the pressure of other po-tential buyers looking over your left shoulder with checkbooks in hand.

7. The once-a-decade "right time at the right place and price" buy.

It is essential that you investigate the opportunity for an early-bird admission on the set-up day or several hours prior to the opening to the general public on the day of the show. It is a given that the

Bought and sold many times.

show will be "picked" by the dealers on set-up day, but there are some shows and markets that allow the dealers and early birds into the venue simultaneously.

Several years ago, we were at a friend's antiques market before the gates were open to the dealers on Saturday morning at 11 a.m. The line of dealers to get in had formed several hours before, and they were anxious to get inside the gates and unpack. The show opened to the general public on Sunday morning at 8 a.m. Thirty minutes after the gates opened to the dealers, we found a 35" cast-iron eagle that had decorated the entrance to a gas station in Oklahoma or Kansas in the 1920s. We bought the eagle for $850, after a brief period of negotiation. Over the next several hours, two other dealers stopped by and mentioned that they had also owned the eagle that morning and had sold it while waiting in the line.

The point of this short story is that we were the fourth to own the eagle that morning. Keep in mind that was 21 hours before the show opened to the general public at 8 a.m. on Sunday.

Prices and Problems

One of several challenges faced by country and Americana collectors today is determining exactly what to pay for something that catches their attention at an antiques market or show. It is especially a trying experience for collectors who have been in the hunt for 30 years and were weaned on $50 "bird" jugs and $200 painted cupboards.

In a late 1996 issue of the *Maine Antiques Digest*, there was a review of an East Coast antiques show and numerous pictures of merchandise that had been offered for sale. There was a photograph of two Shaker berry buckets that were similar to a hundred we have seen over the years, except these were each priced at more than $1,000. This creates significant sticker-shock for someone who can

This Shaker berry bucket should be classified as "uncommon," not "rare."

remember comparable buckets in the $50-$100 range.

It is important to remember that these buckets were made in quantity for sale in the gift or tourist shops at Eastern Shaker communities in the late 19th and early 20th centuries. They are staved, painted and encircled with metal bands and diamond-shaped braces at the handle. They are found in several sizes ranging to about

Do you remember when tins like this sold for a song?

8" in diameter. They would be classified, even by today's inflated standards, as more "uncommon" than "rare."

In the 1970s and 1980s, when the painted-surface mania began to blossom, most collectors had at least an idea about how much to pay for a particular piece, because they routinely saw similar examples and had a standard of comparison. That is no longer the case today, because the demand for rare and upper-end merchandise is far greater than the supply of legitimate examples offered at auctions, shows or markets.

As prices have risen, many collectors have been forced to redefine and adjust the way they accumulate Americana. For example, some stoneware collectors have begun to limit their search to specific potteries or types of stoneware (vendors' jugs, one-gallon ovoids, batter jugs) rather than attempting to purchase everything that appeals to them, because it is prohibitively expensive in today's market.

It is also important to understand that Americana collectors 30 years ago could buy without a great deal of knowledge, because reproductions of painted surfaces were almost nonexistent, and there was not enough interest yet to create a market for new stoneware, baskets or textiles to be disguised as old and offered for sale. Unfortunately, today it takes time, money and knowledge to build a collection.

We have gotten a significant number of letters and telephone calls over the years from people with questions about something they were given, inherited, found, bought or tripped over. Invariably, the items have some kind of relationship to their geographic locale, and we can honestly tell them it probably has more value within 50 miles of where they are sitting, standing or lying than anywhere else on the planet.

The candy container made to appear as a miniature lunch pail was sold at Kitchell's Candy in Bloomington, Ill., between 1915 and the 1930s (when the business flourished). The tin is worth three to four times more in Bloomington, than in San Francisco or Portland, Maine. You can call this phenomenon "Raycraft's Rule of Geographic Proximity." It hasn't been trademarked or registered yet, so feel free to use it anyway you want.

Pickers

A picker is an individual in the antiques business who often anonymously goes from auctions to tag sales to isolated antiques shops looking for anything that has "a few dollars left in it" to sell to dealers who bump the price and offer it to their retail customers.

Most pickers like to deal with a relatively small group of dealers, because they know what the dealers are looking for and the prices they can pay. The dealers usually like to see the picker show up at their shops because they never know what will be under the tarp in the back of the van or truck. Pickers also have the time and knowledge to get into buying situations that most dealers will never encounter.

Over the years, we have come into contact with several pickers and each was unique in his or her approach to the antiques business. One gentleman knew very little about antiques, but he possessed the rare and highly desirable "good eye." He often didn't know what something was, but he instinctively knew it was good. It made no difference if it was a piece of redware or carnival glass. The more serious and successful pickers often mix a fertile memory and extensive resource library with the "good eye."

Q&A with John Colteaux: Picking the Mind of a Picker

John Colteaux is a Bloomington, Ill.-based antiques picker who combines knowledge, mobility, an extensive resource library and the rare "good eye" into a successful business.

Q. How do you define the term "picker" today?

A. A person with vast knowledge of antiques and collectibles who buys from various sources and generally sells quickly and quietly to dealers.

Q. How has the job of the "picker" changed in recent years?

A. It is extremely difficult in today's market to buy items that are experiencing popularity, due to the large number of price guides available. Therefore, it is nearly impossible to buy Roseville, Hull, etc.

Q. How wide a geographic area do you cover?

A. 150-mile radius of Bloomington/Normal, Ill.

Q. It takes a great deal of knowledge to be a picker. What kinds of things are you most comfortable with when you buy?

A. Pieces with unique style, one-of-a-kind or rare items, high quality pieces.

Q. What was your all-time greatest find?

A. A Steigel flask in daisy and hexagon pattern, purchased for $600 and worth approximately $10,000.

Q. What was your all-time biggest mistake?

A. A few reproductions amounting to a couple hundred dollars in loss.

Q. How do you keep yourself aware of sales, auctions and so forth?

A. *Antique Weekly*, auctioneers' flyers, newspapers, word of mouth.

Road Trip Information

Newspapers

The following 10 antiques newspapers will probably send you a sample copy if you call:

1. *Antiques and the Arts Weekly*
   (203) 426-8036

2. *Antiques & Auction News*
   (717) 653-9797

3. *Art & Antiques Northeast*
   800-274-7594

4. *The Hudson Valley Antiquer*
   (914) 876-8766

5. *Maine Antiques Digest*
   800-752-8521

6. *New England Antiques Journal*
   (413) 967-3505

7. *New York Antique Almanac*
   (212) 988-2700

8. *New York-Pennsylvania Collector*
   800-836-1868

9. *Renninger's Antique Guide*
   (610) 828-4614

10. *Western Connecticut & Western Massachusetts Antiquer*
    (914) 876-8766

Lodging & Dining

Here are the phone numbers for nine motel/hotel chains you might want to consider using on your road trip:

1. Comfort Inns: 800-228-5150

2. Days Inns: 800 325-2525

3. Fairfield Inns: 800-228-2800

4. Hampton Inns: 800-HAMPTON

5. Holiday Inns: 800-HOLIDAY

6. Ramada Inns: 800-228-2828

7. Red Roof Inns: 800-THE-ROOF

8. Shoney's Inns: 800-222-2222

9. Signature Inns: 800-822-5252

Three of our all-time favorite restaurants:

Monell's: 1235 6th Ave. North, Nashville, TN 37208, (615) 248-4747

The Hopkins' House: 900 N. Spring St. Pensacola, FL (904) 438-3979.

Monell's and The Hopkins' House are two legendary Southern family-style restaurants that don't take reservations and seat your party with the first space available around communal tables. The dishes of Southern stables are enhanced with a nightly special of food you probably haven't eaten for awhile, but will yearn for again. The Hopkins' House may be the only restaurant in the United States closed on Saturday and Sunday evenings and all day on Monday.

Tobin's Pizza Restaurant: 1513 N. Main Bloomington, IL, (309) 828-0410

An archtypical Midwestern pizza parlor with an extensive menu and the best French dressing in North America.

21 Vocabulary Words to Study

(Trial test on Tuesday/final test on Friday)

1. *Architectural*: Term used to describe a cupboard or chest that was built into a house. It could also be a structural part of a building (post, window, trim, mantel, etc.) that has been removed.

2. *As found*: Offered in the same condition as when it was taken from the basement, barn or loft where it was discovered, uncleaned and as-is.

3. *Attribution*: The process of assigning a probable maker to a particular piece of Americana based on its design, color, method of construction or comparison to previously known examples.

4. *Brimfield*: Massachusetts community on Rt. 20, east of Springfield, that hosts three huge antiques markets in the spring, summer and fall each year that draw thousands of dealers and collectors.

5. *Brown furniture*: A term often used to describe an antiques event or booth that did not contain much painted fur-

niture, but had an abundance of cherry, walnut and mahogany.

6. *Buyer's premium*: An additional cost (usually 10% to 20%) added on to the price of an item purchased at auction.

7. *Case piece*: A piece of furniture framed like a box. Examples are cupboards, desks and chests of drawers.

8. *Decorator stuff*: Usually a negative term to describe merchandise that would not interest serious collectors, but is attractive to individuals seeking a distinctive look. Decorator stuff is purchased by those who are less concerned about authenticity than appearance.

9. *Early buyer (early bird)*: An individual who pays an early admission fee to a preview, set-up or opportunity to shop before a show or market is open to the general public. The fee can range from $10 to more than $100.

10. *Heart*: Heart of the Country is an antiques show held in the fall and winter at the Opry Land Hotel complex in Nashville. Several tailgate shows, within walking distance, bring serious collectors from across the nation.

11. *MAD*: The Maine Antiques Digest is probably the most influential monthly newspaper read by Americana collectors.

12. *Married* : The unhappy mating of two pieces of furniture that share some design characteristics. A cupboard bottom that has lost its upper section somewhere along the way can be reborn when a cupboard top without a bottom is matched to it. The trick is match the finish of the surfaces of both pieces.

13. *Merch*: A term often used by dealers to describe the very average offerings in their booths. "It's just merch."

14. *Overpainted*: Describes the surface of a piece of furniture that contains several coats of paint accumulated over the years.

15. *Painted wooden fragments*: A relatively new area of Americana collecting where pieces of furniture with unique decoration are offered for sale. These fragments of furniture may include a crest rail from a chair, a head board from a bed and so forth. They are mounted and displayed like a piece of sculpture.

16. *Patina*: The surface appearance of a piece of furniture (or other item) caused by exposure over time to human contact, dust, weather, sunlight and bumps and bruises.

17. *Picked*: An antiques show or market is described as "picked" if dealers and early buyers have had an opportunity to make purchases prior to the opening to the general public. The "picking" takes place most often while the dealers are setting up their booths.

18. *Pieced out*: Chairs and tables that have lost height because of exposure to the weather or a wet basement occasionally have several inches added to their legs to restore them to their original dimensions. The problem can arise of matching the old paint with the newly added pieced-out portion of the piece.

19. *Provenance*: Refers to the history of ownership of a given piece of Americana.

20. *Right*: If a piece of furniture is described as "right," it suggests that it is in its original condition with no significant additions or subtractions.

21. *Smalls*: A dealer whose booth is filled with pieces of pottery, baskets, buttermolds and wooden bowls can be described as having smalls.

Organizing a Collection

Our good friends, Bobby and Judy Farling, have organized their collection by designing 5" by 7" file cards with all the necessary information. They also clip or staple a color photograph of the piece and the original receipt for its purchase to the back of the card. The key is to place the cards in a place that is not accessible to burst pipes in January or the threat of destruction by fire.

Here are several pertinent pieces of information you might want to put on the card:

1. Name of item and description (including age/period, provenance, size/dimensions, origin/maker's mark and condition)

2. Price paid and appraised value

3. Address and phone number of person you purchased the item from

4. Where and when you purchased the item

You might also wish to consider one of several computer software packages that are aimed at keeping track of your collection.

CHAPTER 4
IN THE KITCHEN

Kitchen and Hearth Antiques

(Note: This chapter was prepared by Teri and Joe Dziadul. It illustrates items from their personal collection. The Dziaduls have been filling special requests for more than 25 years and offer kitchen and hearth antiques for sale to collectors and dealers. The current list of items for sale may be obtained by sending $1 to the Dziaduls at 6 S. George Washington Rd., Enfield, CT 06082.)

The wide hearths and huge chimneys that characterized 18th century New England kitchens pulled vast drafts of air throughout the house, while little heat actually warmed the room. The building of the morning fire was an architectural achievement. Atop this arrangement was a pyramid of smaller fragments, properly positioned with spaces for the blaze. Small beds of glowing coals served to provide more even-controlled heat for footed skillets and pots. Even though cast iron cracked (the blacksmith patched and riveted pots) seldom was a piece so damaged that it was discarded.

Over the fireplace, a deep cupboard held whale-oil lamps, flatirons, iron kitchen utensils—necessary essentials for daily living. On an opposite wall stood a dresser with open shelves and rails on which to rest the edges of pewter plates. Leaning forward in this manner, their surface was protected from dust. These plates, bright as polished silver, captured the flicker of the firelight and reflected the flame.

The aroma of ripening apples in the cellar and herbs drying above the hearth mingled with that of the spacious store closet each time the door was opened. In her history journal, Ruth Huntington Sessions recalls, "The moment Grandmother turned the key in the door, one perceived a fragrance, exotic and rare; a mixture of spices, fruits, syrups, nuts—words cannot describe the richness of that mixture, the product of age—old sweetness to which Europe and Asia had contributed and which seemed to cling to the very walls and shelves, immaculate though they were." Here stood rows of preserves, miniature casks of tamarinds, flat boxes of guava jelly, round-shouldered blue jars enclosed in a network of split bamboo and filled with fiery ginger, chests of green and black tea "with queer little Chinamen with long queues hanging down behind," bags of Java and mocha coffee, boxes of Malaga raisins, drums of figs, casks of grapes, jugs of molasses, and cones of purple cloaked sugar, "their bright-colored labels fastened with little bows of red ribbon."

Pound cakes, custards, gingerbread and puddings were baked on the hearth in a Dutch oven. Minced, apple, pumpkin and chicken pies were baked in a brick oven, large enough to hold a dozen pies.

At the end of the 18th century, tin kitchens became popular; a spit could be fixed at regular intervals around a 360-degree axis for directing heat where it was most needed and to avoid singeing wing-tips and other tender areas. Prior to this, meat was roasted on a spit, resting on brackets of the high iron andirons. Inspired by the Industrial Revolution in the middle of the 19th century, growing technology produced many simple and some complex labor-saving gadgets. The following pages exhibit fine examples of both styles.

To acquire kitchen and hearth collectibles, permit your lifetime to be your timetable. There are many elusive rarities that will require this time-frame. Buy examples that you love and never hesitate when a scarce object is discovered. You may never have that opportunity again at any price. Consider not only the financial aspect in collecting, but the priceless benefits invested in your own happiness.

Acknowledgments: Many thanks to Chuck and Bonnie Badger, Carol Bohn, Bob Cahn and Phyllis and Jim Moffet who shared their collections at a recent convention of Kollectors of Old Kitchenware.

Importance of the Apple

Edward Everett Hale, one of America's great writers, penned a note from his childhood, testifying to the importance of the apple in 19th century New England: "I remember that in more than one winter, when my grandmother in Westhampton had sent us a keg or two of home apple-sauce, the sloop which brought the treasure was frozen up in the Connecticut River below Hartford, so that it was four or five months before we hungry children enjoyed her present."

H.B. Stowe Writes About Apples

Harriet Beecher Stowe invoked the importance of apples in New England as she writes in the early 1800s of her childhood in Litchfield, Conn. "There were several occasions in course of the yearly housekeeping requiring every hand in the house, which would have lagged sadly had it not been for father's inspiring talent. One of these was the apple-cutting season, in the autumn, when a barrel of cider apple-sauce had to be made, which was to stand frozen in the milkroom, and cut out from time to time in red glaciers, which when duly thawed, supplied the table. The work was done in the kitchen, an immense brass kettle hanging over the deep fireplace, a bright fire blazing and snapping, and all hands, children and servants, employed on the full baskets of apples and quinces that stood around. I have the image of my father still as he sat working the apple peeler."

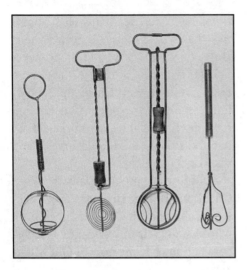

From left: Known to collectors as "The Loll," patented by Frederick W. Loll of Meriden, Conn., in 1906 ($475-$575); Dover coil-bottom beater, c1870 ($575-$675); Vortex, Patent Model ($800-$900).

From left: Archimedes-Principle whippers—no identification, but patented by James R. Hughes of Saugus, Mass., all wire ($300-$400); Dudley-Bryant ($275-$375); no identification, known as "Improved Rapid" ($375-$475); no identification, known as "MacKay" ($375-$475).

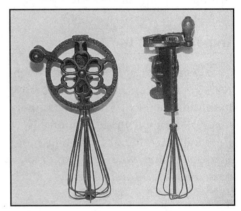

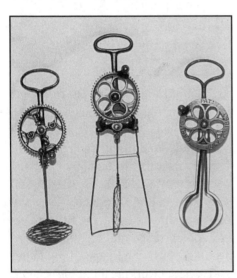

From left: Monroe Mfg. Co., Fitchburg, Mass., Beater ($850-$1,000); Monitor Beater, patented by Moses G. Crane of Boston ($1,200-$1,400).

From left: P-D and Co., beater, c1885 ($900-$1,000); Express beater, c1887, often referred to as the "fly swatter beater" ($1,000-$1,200); Earl's Patent Beater, 1863 ($450-$550).

Combination Syllabub churn, rolling pin, reamer, sieve, apple corer, cookie cutter, funnel ($850-$950).

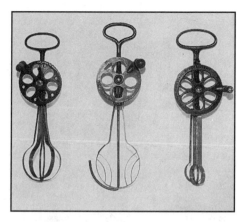

From left: Dover beater, 1903 ($45-$55); standard egg beater ($375-$475); Dover tumbler beater with small dashers for mixing in tumblers or glasses ($100-$150).

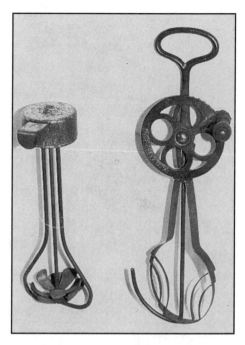

From left: Korena egg and cream whipper, New York, N.Y. ($275-$325); standard beater ($375-$475).

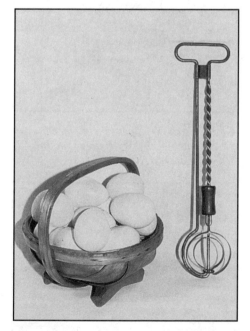

From left: Trug basket ($95-$125); glass and porcelain eggs ($12-$15 each); Bryant beater by Charles Bryant of Wakefield, Mass., c1885 ($245-$300).

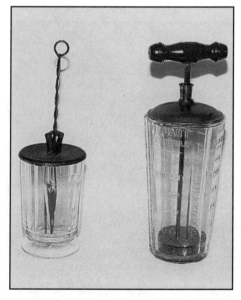

From left: Keystone egg and cream beater, Westmoreland Spec. Co., Grapeville, Pa. ($175-$195); Silver & Co., beater jar ($175-$200).

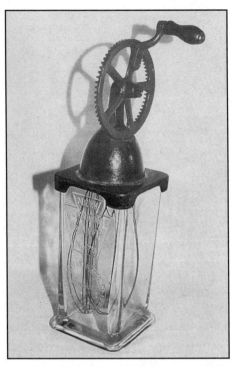

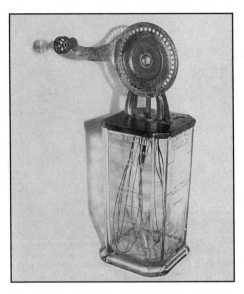

New Keystone beater jar, Culinary Utilities Co., New York, N.Y., Bloomfield, N.J. ($225-$250).

New Keystone beater jar, No. 20, Pat. Dec. 15, 1885, cast-iron top and wire whisk dashers ($325-$350).

Globe Glass Whipper, metal mechanical parts, patented by W. Helmer on June 7, 1904 ($1,100-$1,200).

S&S Hutchinson mayo jar, embossed "S&S, 852 Vernon Ave., Long Island City" ($350-$400).

Delft mayonnaise mixer, china bowl, metal top with S-shaped beater and oil funnel with shut-off lever ($450-$500).

22

Lightning 1-quart butter churn, quart sizes command higher prices ($250-$300).

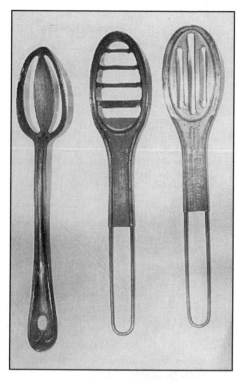

From left: Tin beater spoons—The Eugenia Kilborn, pat. 1884, Rumford cake mixer and cream whip ($30-$35); Rumford cake mixer, cream whip and egg beater ($30-$35).

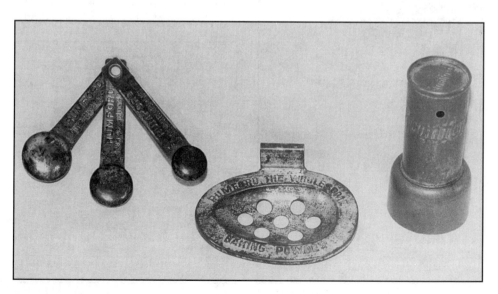

From left: Rumford items—tin measuring spoons ($55-$68); spoon rest, hooks on side of pot ($85-$150); biscuit cutter ($15-$25).

Mounted sugar cutters on iron base, scarce version, most cutters are secured to wood bases ($575-$675).

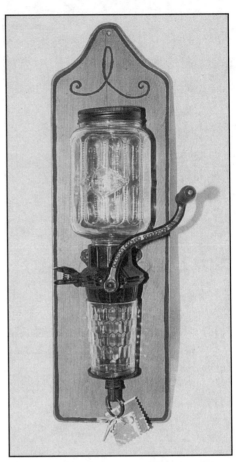

Freidac Mfg. Co. coffee mill ($300-$400).

Wilmot Castle Company coffee mill ($275-$325).

Flour sifter, cast-iron frame, St. Louis maker ($575-$675).

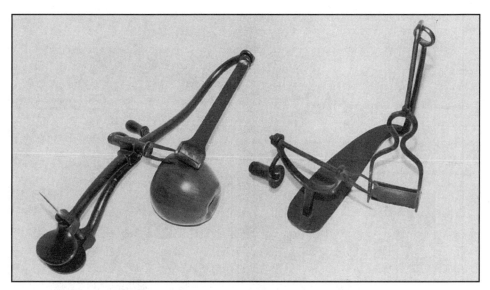

Wrought-iron apple parers, c1820-40 ($550-$650).

From left: Cast-iron meat tenderizer, "Pat. Apld. For" in casting ($75-$100); cast-iron meat tenderizer, marked "Lee's Meat Tenderizer. Pat. Applied For" ($150-$200).

Ice cream penny licks, penny and tuppeny sizes, predecessors of the ice cream cone ($65-$95); ice cream scoop, Mason Magic Scoop, Boston, aluminum ($35-$45).

Champion apple parer, automatic parer, slicer and corer ($550-$650).

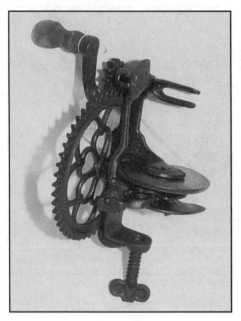

Waverly apple parer, c1884 ($275-$325).

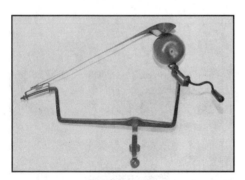

Wrought-iron apple parer, c1820-40 ($650-$750).

Davis apple slicer, Patented March 13, 1834, very scarce version ($1,000-$1,200).

Favorite apple parer, Mf'd by L.A. Sayre, Newark, N.J. ($275-$325).

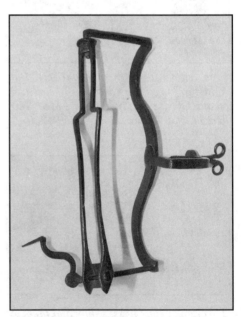

Wrought-iron apple parer, c1820-40, very scarce version, double ram's horn serpentine-style ($700-$800).

Tin apple-related items—Combination strainer, cookie cutter, doughnut cutter, apple corer ($35-$55); combination grater, slicer, peeler and corer ($45-$75); Silvers apple segmenter ($75-$95); apple corer ($35-$45).

Apple segmenters ($75-$125).

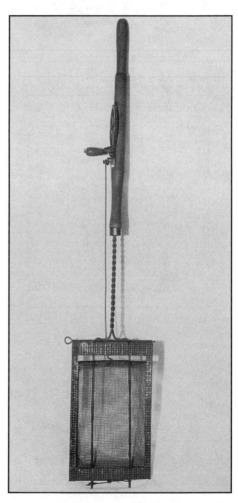

Turntable '98 apple parer, made by Goodell Co., Antrim, N.H., ($85-$125).

Mechanical corn popper, Quincy Hardware Co., Ill., Pat. May 24, 1892 ($650-$750).

Combination grater and cookie cutter ($650-$750).

From left: Miniature candle molds, 6-1/2" high round mold, marked "Mason's" ($1,000-$1,200); 5" high mold ($650-$750).

Japanned spice holder and nutmeg grater, two levels of spice containers ($1,000-$1,200).

Miniature candle molds, about 5" tall ($675-$800).

Tin candle mold, stretcher base ($450-$550).

Raisin seeder, The Magic, Antrim, N.H. ($650-$750).

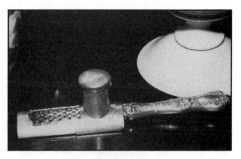

Sterling mechanical nutmeg grater, Pat. June 29, '97 ($1,000-$1,200).

Tin candle mold, 16 tubes surrounded by a wall structure, scarce ($675-$750).

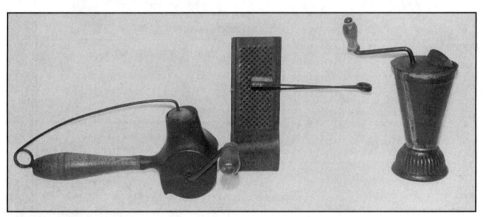

Mechanical nutmeg graters, all scarce versions ($700-$1,000).

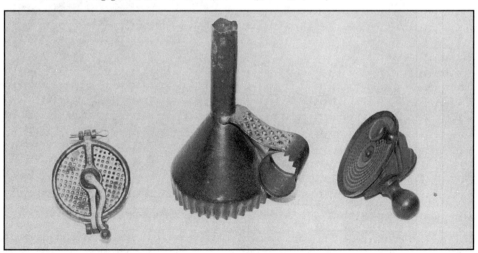

From left: Mechanical nutmeg grater ($750-$850); combination cookie cutter, funnel, candleholder and grater ($600-$650); mechanical nutmeg grater ($850-$950).

Asparagus buncher, E. Watts, Keyport, N.J., Pat. Dec. 6, 1887 ($150-$250).

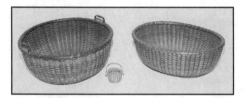

From left: Nantucket baskets—7-1/2" diameter, round basket ($500-$600); 7-1/2" long oval basket ($500-$600); miniature swing-handle basket ($400-$450).

Tin-and-wood flour sifter ($275-$375).

Cabbage slicer, scarce version ($250-$350).

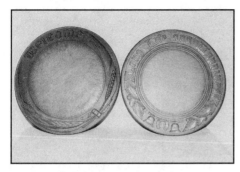

From left: Bread boards—welcome board ($250-$275); wedding board ($375-$500).

Peaseware pedestal urns, for storage of thimbles or pill boxes ($300-$500).

From left: Yellow ware bowl, smaller sizes are found less frequently ($55-$75); Yellow ware frog, scarce ($80-$95).

Pottery rolling pins—bittersweet bands ($650-$750); blue onion pin ($350-$400).

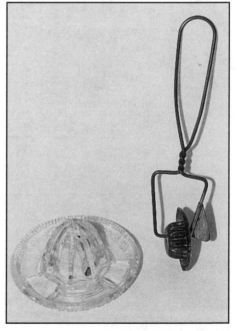

From left: Lemon reamer, Easley's Pat. July 10, 1888, Sep. 10, 1889 ($45-$55); pastry tool, pie prick, cutter and crimper, Pat. March 10, '08 ($85-$95).

Wood herb crusher ($550-$650).

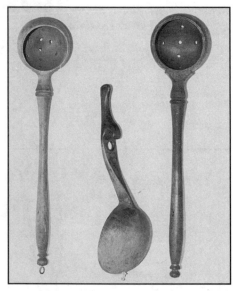

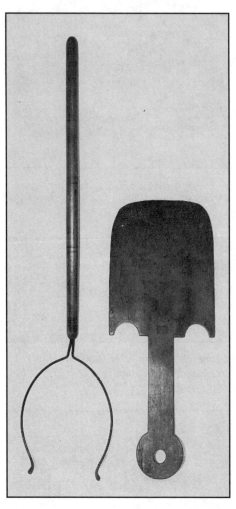

From left: Wood strainers ($125-$175); carved wood ladle ($275-$375).

From left: Pie peels, iron tines, wood handle ($150-$200); 18th century wood peel ($200-$300).

Wire bakery display tray ($75-$125).

Peter Ompir painted trays, unusual golf scenes ($275-$375 each).

From left: Tin ABC cup ($125-$150); tin ABC covered pail ($225-$275).

Tin ABC plates ($165-$275).

From left: Make-do's: Chinese export teapot, tin reinforcement ($350-$400); goblet, wood base ($100-$125).

From left: Glass candy jars—ground stopper, 12" high jar ($95-$125); ground stopper, 27" high jar ($400-$475). In country stores, gleaming glass jars held gumdrops, peppermints, rock candy, non-pareils, candy-coated peanuts (Boston Baked Beans), licorice and taffy whips and chewable wax bottles filled with sweet liquids. Among the favorites with children were the conversation lozenges or cockle (shell-shaped candies made of sugar and flour, in which slips of colored paper were inserted with jokes and fortunes).

Miniature tin plates ($175-$475).

Tin baby's rattles ($150-$200).

From left: Make-do's—toby mug, tin strap handle ($350-$450); Chinese export mug, wrought-iron handle ($325-$375); glass goblet, tin base ($65-$95).

Tin biscuit oven, used on the hearth for baking biscuits which, in those early days of tin ovens, were made of corn meal—also known as Indian Meal—and water ($450-$550).

Miniature tin apple roaster, scarce, salesman sample ($450-$500).

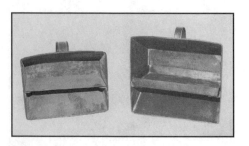

Miniature biscuit ovens, very likely a tinsmith's sales sample, rare ($400-$450).

From left: Egg-related items—egg candler ($175-$200); pottery egg separator ($65-$85); scarce egg baking powder, biscuit cutter ($375-$475); glass egg separators ($200-$250).

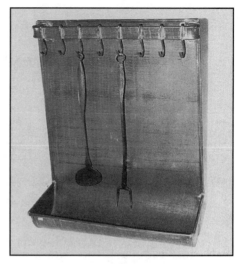

Tin hanging utensil rack ($400-$500); iron spatula ($65-$85); iron fork ($55-$75).

Lemon squeezer, all wood on wooden base ($350-$450).

Miniature Shaker sewing basket ($500-$600).

Pie crimpers ($75-$200).

CHAPTER 5
STONEWARE

Decorated American Stoneware Today

(This state-of-the-stoneware market was prepared by Bruce Waasdorp)

Decorated American stoneware is a booming collector field. An appreciation of this important part of our culture and history has brought about a renewed interest in this uniquely American folk-art category. Today, the majority of collectors are enthused with the many examples of cobalt designs and utilitarian shapes. Many preference their choices into categories. They may collect specific factory marks or types of designs, such as birds or flowers. As an example, one collector displays only 2-gallon jugs with flower designs. Others may collect only dated pieces, advertising marks, state-of-origin pieces or miniature pottery. The possibilities truly are endless.

Although it is not a guarantee for the future, current prices of stoneware are on the rise. Remember, thousands of pieces were produced by numerous factories for more than 100 years. But since they were originally inexpensive, easily replaced and not considered potential heirlooms, relatively little remains today. Stoneware was not originally intended as an elegant art object. It was utilitarian and used daily, as well as admired. Today, this once household necessity now complements and accents the decor of early American to modern home interiors.

Prices currently range from $50 to $50,000. Rarity of design, size, condition and maker can all enhance the value, as with any other antique or collectible. There is a remarkable range of variations available and each is desirable in its own right. The most important aspect of collecting American folk art is to enjoy your stoneware.

Notes on Collecting Decorated Stoneware

1. The value of a piece of stoneware is primarily a factor of how elaborately it has been decorated. Other primary factors include condition, form, maker, color of the clay and size of the piece.

2. Stoneware collecting is such a specialized category of Americana that the best buys often are from dealers who specialize in it. Our experience is that dealers who only periodically acquire a heavily decorated piece tend to overprice it, because they are unfamiliar with the market.

3. Serious folk-art and stoneware collectors often face-off at auctions when a spectacularly decorated example surfaces. This confrontation tends to inflate prices and fuels the market.

4. After you purchase a piece of stoneware, make it a point to receive, from the dealer, a detailed receipt that accurately describes it. This can become even more meaningful after you get it home and find a repair that was not previously noted by you or the seller.

5. There is a wealth of mediocre stoneware in the market place that has changed little in demand or value over the past decade. Unusual examples command serious attention and dollars and will continue to escalate in value and demand.

6. There is growing interest by regional collectors in acquiring examples of stoneware made within their limited geographic area. For example, uncommon pieces of Peoria Pottery are significantly more valuable within 100 miles of Peoria than anywhere else in the world.

7. The value of heavily decorated 19th century pieces of stoneware have a universal value that has no geographic limitations The rare cobalt-decorated Peoria jug that would cause hearts to flutter in Illinois would create little interest at an antiques show in Boston or Boise. A cobalt cornucopia on a Bennington jug would result in serious checks being written in San Francisco or Chicago.

8. Contemporary stoneware decorated with cobalt birds and flowers normally should not create too many problems for collectors, because the pieces tend to be lighter in weight and thinner in construction.

9. The "fake" stoneware that can be a potential concern is an undecorated 19th century jug or crock with cobalt decoration added in 1991. There is almost an unlimited supply of 19th century stoneware still available that was not originally decorated. Eventually, this could present a problem for collectors who buy emotionally and not intellectually.

Sources

One of the few Americana antiques dealers who specializes in decorated stoneware is Stephen Rhodes. Rhodes is a respected stoneware dealer who consistently maintains an inventory of more than 300 pieces. He may be reached in Champaign, Il at, (217) 356-4612.

Four Stoneware Books You Need

1. Greer, Georgeanna, *American Stonewares: The Art and Craft of Utilitarian Potters* (Atglen, PA: Schiffer Publishing, 1961).

2. Guilland, Harold, *Early American Folk Pottery* (Radnor, PA: Chilton Book Company, 1971).

3. Osgood, Cornelius, *The Jug and Related Stoneware of Bennington* (Rutland, VT: Charles L. Tuttle Company, 1971).

4. Webster, Donald, *Decorated Stoneware Potter of North America* (Rutland, VT: Charles L. Tuttle Company, 1971).

Stoneware at Auction

Vicki and Bruce Waasdorp have conducted semi-annual decorated stoneware auctions by mail and telephone for several years. Prior to each auction, they issue a fully illustrated catalog for collectors to study. Each piece of stoneware offered for sale in the auction is pictured and described in detail.

Collectors may use the mail, fax or telephone to make their bids, with a specific time-frame. Following the auction, each catalog subscriber receives a prices-realized listing. Even if you don't pick up a piece of stoneware through the Waasdorp auction, the catalog serves as the most accurate and updated price guide to stoneware that is currently available to collectors. For information about future auctions contact Vicki and Bruce Waasdorp, P.O. Box 434, 10931 Main St., Clarence, NY 14031, (716) 759-2361.

The pictures, descriptions and prices that follow were provided by the Waasdorps from their Oct. 6, 1996, auction (prices listed include a 10% buyer's premium; prices were rounded to the nearest $5):

From left: Unsigned, 1-gallon jar with bird and "one" in blue script, original lid, 5" tight through-line on side, 10" high, c1870 ($470); L. & B.G. Chace, Somerset, 1-gallon squat jug with brush-blue "spitting" flower, minor glaze spider in the back, 10-1/2" high, c1860 ($220).

From left: West Troy Pottery, 1-gallon jug, dated 1876, professional restoration to flaking around the base, 12" high ($220); West Troy Pottery, 2-gallon jug with leaf decoration, minor surface chip at spout and 4" very tight line on one side, 14" high, c1870 ($145).

From left: S. Hart, 1-gallon jug with "1" framed in brush-blue plume, 5" tight through-line on side at base, 10-1/2" high, c1870 ($145); Albany, N.Y., 1-gallon jug with long-tailed bird, hairline in handle, 11-1/2" high, c1870 ($300).

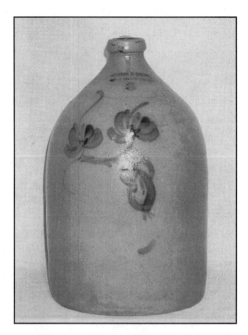

Norton & Fenton, East Bennington, Vt., 2-gallon jug with triple flower, very minor stone ping on the side, 13-1/2" high, c1860 ($275).

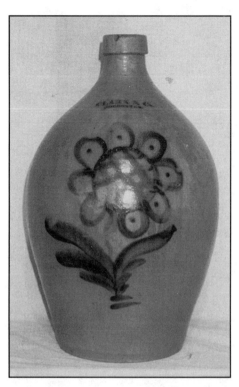

Clark and Company, Rochester, 3-gallon jug with large flower, some age-staining, spout chip and stack-mark, 16-1/2" high, c1840 ($605).

J. Fisher, Lyons, N.Y., 3-gallon jug with "3" accented, excellent, 15-1/2" high, c1885 ($165).

From left: Whites, Utica, N.Y., 1-gallon jug with pine-tree decoration, minor chip on spout from use, 12" high, c1865 ($190); Whites, Utica, N.Y., 1-gallon jar with flamingo design and lid, two minor surface chips at base, 9-1/2" high, c1865 ($330).

From left: New York Stoneware Co., Ft. Edward, N.Y., 1-gallon jug with large bird on twig decoration, some staining, spout chips, age-lines in handle and large glaze drip on side, 11-1/2" high, c1870 ($305); New York Stoneware Co., 2-gallon crock with leaf design, minor surface wear on interior rim and 2" tight line on the back, 9-1/2" high, c1865 ($165).

From left: Unsigned, 1-gallon ovoid jug with brush-flower decoration, some over-glazing and minor stack-mark, 12" high, c1840 ($130); Lyons 1-gallon preserve jar with flower and blue accents at ears, professional restoration to rim chip in front, 10" high, c1860 ($210).

From left: Ballard & Brothers, Burlington, Vt., 2-gallon ovoid crock with dark-blue flower, minor kiln burn, 10" high, c1860 ($250); Nichols & Boynton, Burlington, Vt., 1-gallon jug with brush double flower, spout chip and chip at base on the side, 12" high, c1855 ($145).

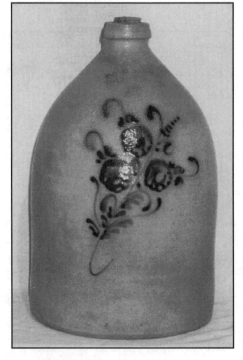

J. & E. Norton, Bennington, Vt., 2-gallon jug with triple floral plume, surface chip at spout, 14-1/2" high, c1855 ($415).

John Burger, Rochester, N.Y., 3-gallon jug with triple-fern decoration, 16-1/2" high, c1865 ($360).

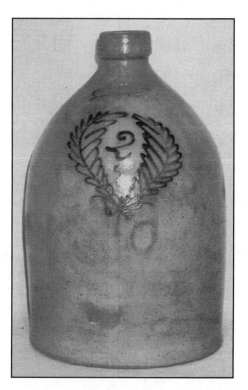

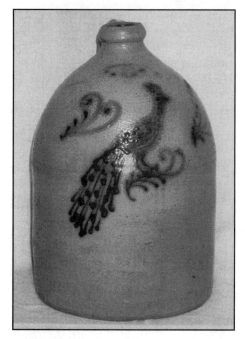

Burger & Co., Rochester, 2-gallon jug with signature wreath design, overall staining, 13-1/2" high, c1879 ($145).

L. Seymour, Troy, N.Y., 3-gallon jug with large and rare peacock design, stone ping and stack-mark in the making, 15" high, c1850 ($660).

From left: Unsigned, 1-gallon advertising jug, overall staining and a small surface chip at spout, 12" high, c1880 ($120); unsigned, bristol glaze 1-gallon advertising jug with dark-blue stenciling, surface chip at base and at spout, 11" high, c1890 ($210).

41

Whites, Utica, N.Y., 3-gallon jug with leaf and orchid decoration, dark blue, 17" high, c1865 ($275).

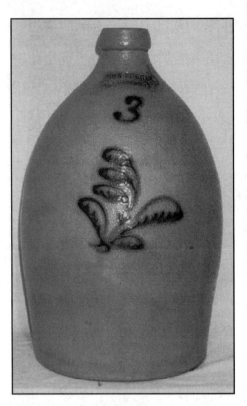

John Burger, Rochester, 3-gallon jug with triple-bud flower, excellent condition, 16" high, c1860 ($385).

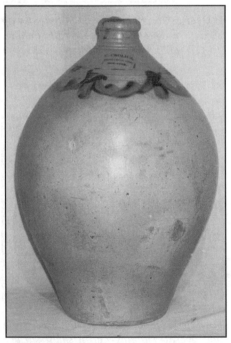

C. Crolium Manufacturer, New York, 3-gallon ovoid jug with brush-swag design, some overall glaze wear from use and some staining in back, 17" high, c1840 ($690).

From left: Unsigned, 2-gallon ovoid jug with blue-stripe accents, possibly from Ohio, stack-mark on the side, 13" high, c1850 ($155); unsigned, 2-gallon ovoid jug with brush flower and original carved wooden stopper, stack-mark in front, design fry and minor stone pings in the making, 14" high, c1820 ($220).

From left: Boynton & Co., Troy, N.Y., 2-gallon jug with "316" in blue cobalt on front, unusual advertising piece, large stone ping on the back, 13" high, c1825 ($220); N.A. Seymour, Rome, 2-gallon ovoid jug with brushed "2" and blue accent at name and handle, professional restoration to age-lines at base, 13" high, c1890 ($130).

From left: John Burger, Rochester, N.Y., 2-gallon jug with slip- and brush-flower design, chip at the base on the side, 13" high, c1885 ($200); Burger & Lang, Rochester, N.Y., 2-gallon jug with double-bud flower, spider age-line and glaze-flake on back, 14-1/2" high, c1870 ($175).

From left: J. Burger Jr., Rochester, N.Y., 2-gallon jug with hops design, minor spider age-line in the glaze, 13-1/2" high, c1885 ($220); Burger & Lang, Rochester, N.Y., 2-gallon jug with "X" in blue cobalt, 15" high, c1870 ($440).

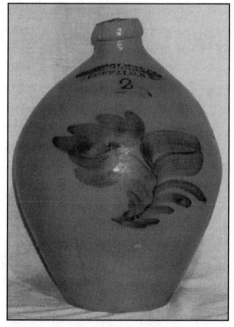

P. Mugler & Co., Buffalo, N.Y., 2-gallon jug with large brush flower, rare mark, surface chip at spout and stack-mark in the making, 12-1/2" high, c1850 ($415).

C.W. Braun, Buffalo, N.Y., 2-gallon jug with large slip- and ribbed-flower decoration, surface chip at spout, 13-1/2" high, c1860 ($495).

N.A. White & Son, Utica, N.Y., 2-gallon jug with paddletail bird, unusual and rare with dotted wings extended, two minor flak-spots and a 3" age-line in the front, 14-1/2" high, c1885 ($2,420).

C.W. Braun, Buffalo, N.Y. 3-gallon jug with dotted and ribbed-flower decoration in dark and heavy blue cobalt, surface chip at spout and glued breaks in handle 16" high, c1860 ($990).

Unsigned, approximate 2-gallon ovoid jug with incised double flower and two flying birds, 15" high, c1810 ($1,075).

N. Clark, Athens, N.Y., approximate 3-gallon ovoid jug with swag accent at name, some design fry and dry glaze, minor chip at spout, 15" high, c1825 ($175).

H.M. Whitman, Havana, N.Y., 3-gallon jug with brush double-flower decoration in dark-blue cobalt, chip at spout, 15-1/2" high, c1860 ($250).

Charlestown, 3-gallon ovoid jug with ochre glaze accent at the top and three diamond-shaped tool marks to signify gallons, professional restoration to handle and some glaze spidering, 17" high, c1820 ($110).

Whites, Utica, N.Y., 3-gallon jug with fat bird on a twig, some glaze run at the shoulder and slightly misshapen, both in the making, 15" high, c1865 ($440).

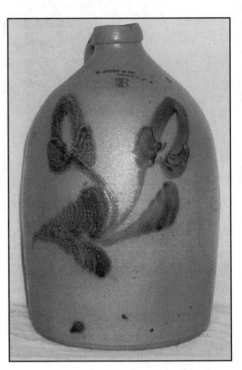

Signed but illegible, 2-gallon jug with slip-tornado design, 14" high, c1880 ($200).

G. Ripley & Co., Ithaca, N.Y., 3-gallon jug with double flower, rare two-year mark, bright blue cobalt, 15" high, c1860 ($330).

Macumber & Tannahill, Ithaca, N.Y., 3-gallon crock with unusual double flower, condition is excellent, rare maker's mark, 10" high, c1875 ($495).

O.L. & A.K. Ballard, Burlington, Vt., 3-gallon crock with snowflake decoration, minor surface chip at rim and some bubbling to thick blue design, 10" high, c1860 ($440).

From left: Haxstun Ottman & Company, Fort Edward, N.Y., 1-gallon jug with bird on a twig, quarter-size surface chip at base on back, 11-1/2" high, c1870 ($330); unsigned, 1-1/2-gallon crock with leaf decoration, discoloration in the making and very minor interior surface chip at rim, 8-1/2" high, c1870 ($100).

Whites, Utica, N.Y., 5-gallon crock with running-bird design, some cobalt missing in thick blue, 5" very tight line on the side, over-glazed in the making and extensive interior lime staining, 12-1/2" high, c1865 ($330).

West Troy, N.Y., Pottery, 3-gallon crock with stylized floral decoration, condition is excellent, 10-1/2" high, c1880 ($440).

From left: Unsigned, 1-gallon pitcher with brushed-floral decoration, chip at spout and base, some design fry, 9" high, c1860 ($385); unsigned, 2-gallon crock, few minor glaze-flecks, 8-1/2" high, c1880 ($80).

Ottman Brothers, Ft. Edward, N.Y., 6-gal-lon crock with basket of flowers, many tight through-lines all around, appears to be sta-ble, 12-1/2" high, c1880 ($145).

N. Clark & Co., Lyons, N.Y., 5-gallon crock with triple flower, 5" tight through-line in front and full-length glued cracks on back, 12-1/2" high, c1850 ($130).

From left: Unsigned, 2-gallon crock with stylized-leaf design, possibly Edmonds, minor surface wear at rim, 9" high, c1870 ($130); unsigned, 1-gallon crock with dark-blue spitting flower, 7" high, c1870 ($220).

From left: Whites, Utica, N.Y., 1-gallon crock with slip-decorated oakleaf, minor surface chips at rim and a through-line along base, 7" high, c1865; Whites, Utica, N.Y., 1-gallon jug with orchid design, some minor design fry and very minor surface chips at base, 11" high, c1865 ($190).

From left: Unsigned, 1-gallon advertising jug with distinct pine-tree decoration, heavy blue, chips at spout, 11" high, c1880 ($250); unsigned, 2-gallon crock with brush double-flower decoration, excellent condition, 9" high, c1880 ($250).

Brady & Ryan, Ellenville, N.Y., 4-gallon crock with bird on stump and dog, stabilized 8" crack in front and minor through-lines on back and side, rare double decoration, 11" high, c1880 ($910).

F.B. Norton, Worcester, Mass., 3-gallon crock with double plume and tornado decoration, 6" tight through-line on side and a 5" y-shaped through-line on back, great example of a signature design from this factory, 10" high, c1870 ($175).

From left: Unsigned, 2-gallon crock with bird on branch, two pencil-size stone pings, 9-1/2" high, c1880 ($385); Riedinger & Caire, Poughkeepsie, N.Y., 2-gallon crock with bird on a twig, two through-lines on front at base and two on back at rim, 9-1/2" high, c1870 ($250).

From left: N. Whites, Utica, N.Y., 2-gallon jar with large bird on branch, misshapen in the making, full length stabilized cracks on back and side, 10-1/2" high, c1865 ($220); unsigned, advertising 2-gallon crock with slip-plume design, excellent, 9" high, c1870 ($210).

From left: Lyons 2-gallon jug with brushed-leaf decoration, two minor stone pings in the making, glaze spider on the back, 14" high, c1860 ($165); J. Fisher, Lyons, N.Y., 2-gallon crock with light-blue plume design, excellent condition, 9" high, c1880 ($110).

Unsigned, high pail-shaped 4-gallon crock with triple iris, incised and blued "Butter," probably Ohio, excellent condition, 13-1/2" high, c1850 ($470).

N.A. White & Son, Utica, N.Y., 4-gallon crock with elaborate compote design, professional restoration to surface chips at rim and ear, 11" high, c1885 ($660).

Ottman Brothers & Co., Ft. Edward, N.Y., 5-gallon crock with large fat bird, some staining, otherwise excellent, 12-1/2" high, c1870 ($770).

J. Burger Jr., Rochester, N.Y., 3-gallon crock with oak-leaf decor, professional restoration to rim chip and line on the back and spider age-lines on the back, 10-1/2" high, c1885 ($90).

Unsigned, 3-gallon crock with dark-blue slip-decorated flower, very tight spider age-lines on back, 10-1/2" high, c1870 ($145).

N.A. White & Son, Utica, N.Y., 2-gallon crock with paddletail-bird design, professional restoration to minor rim chip in front, 9" high, c1885 ($305).

From left: Unsigned, 2-gallon crock with elaborate floral decoration, chip at rim in front, 9" high, c1850 ($175); 1-gallon ovoid jar, signed "Meyer," blue swag around the top of this small jar, large chip at the rim, 4" tight through-lines and surface chips around the base, 9" high, c1830 ($130).

New York Stoneware Co., Ft. Edward, N.Y., 2-gallon crock with fat bird on plume, 4" tight line on both sides, 9" high, c1865 ($440).

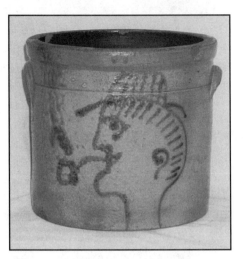

Unsigned, 2-gallon crock with profile of pipe-smoking male, rare decoration, surface chips at rim, base and interior, some glaze run on the left side in the making of the piece, 9" high, c1860 ($1,925).

From left: J. Fisher & Co., Lyons, N.Y., 3-gallon crock with double-tulip decoration in brush design, extremely tight 7" through-line in front, 10" high, c1880 ($120); J. Fisher, 3-gallon crock with brush-plume design, some minor glaze wear and stain spots from use, 10" high, c1880 ($120).

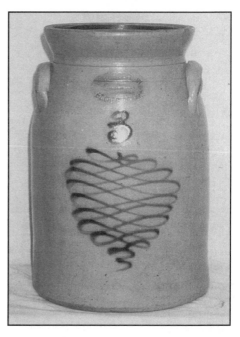

New York Stoneware Co., Ft. Edward, N.Y., 4-gallon jar with rare winged-chicken pecking corn, extensive glaze flaking around the back and sides, 14-1/2" high, c1865 ($855).

J. Burger Jr., Rochester, N.Y., 3-gallon jar with tornado decoration and early wooden churn guide, three surface chips on rim, 4" line on back, unusual high form, 13" high, c1855 ($275).

A.K. Ballard, Burlington, Vt., 4-gallon preserve jar with grape decorations, professional restoration to overall flaking, 14" high, c1860 ($130).

Lyons 2-gallon preserve jar with brilliant blue triple-flower decoration, excellent condition, 11-1/2" high, c1860 ($2,420).

John Burger, Rochester, N.Y., 2-gallon cream pot with large cabbage flower in dark-blue cobalt, long spider age-line on the side, 10-1/2" high, c1865 ($660).

From left: Unsigned, dark-gray ovoid jar with swags and flower designs all around, probably Pennsylvania in origin, minor rim chips, large rim chip in the making, 12" high, c1850 ($200); unsigned, approximate 2-gallon ovoid crock with blue-swag decoration, stack-mark in the blue, excellent condition, 11-1/2" high, c1850 ($100).

Haxstun, Ottman & Co., Ft. Edward, N.Y., 2-gallon ovoid crock with bird on plume, professional restoration to tight lines on back and side, 11" high, c1870 ($210).

From left: Unsigned, 1-gallon preserve jar with blue flower and original lid, lime staining on exterior, 9-1/2" high, c1870 ($155); unsigned, 1-gallon preserve jar with flower and accent at the ears, professional restoration to rim chip, cinnamon cast to glaze in the making of the piece, 5" high, c1860 ($130).

Macumber & Tannahill, Ithaca, N.Y., 4-gallon ovoid crock with flowering-tree design, professional restoration to chips at ears, rim and through-lines on the sides and back, 12" high, c1875 ($165).

John Burger, Rochester, 2-gallon jar with triple-fern decoration, nicely executed, some tight spider age-lines on side and back, 10" high, c1865 ($275).

Cortland, 2-gallon preserve jar with double-flower decoration, artistically shaded, some staining throughout, otherwise excellent, 11" high, c1870 ($220).

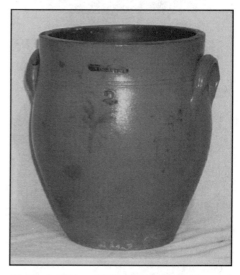

H. Nash, Utica, N.Y, 2-gallon ovoid crock with tree and three-story house and chimney, excellent condition, blue is very light, early mark and rare design, 11" high, c1837 ($385).

J. & E. Norton, Bennington, Vt., 2-gallon jar with heavy blue floral design, two short age-lines up from the base, 11-1/2" high, c1855 ($275).

Edmands & Co., 2-gallon jar with lid and dark-blue floral design, three short and tight age-lines at rim, 12" high, c1870 ($385).

O.L. & A.K. Ballard, Burlington, Vt., 2-gallon preserve jar with "1862" accented with dotted design, glaze-flecks throughout and short, tight line up from base on back, 11" high, c1862 ($415).

Porter & Benedict, 3-gallon cream pot with blue flower, full-length glued crack on back and a large rim chip behind right ear, 13" high, c1850. This piece had an estimated value of $80 in the catalog prior to the auction, but it did not sell.

From left: J. Morton Jordan, 2-gallon ovoid crock with dotted triple-flower decoration, rare mark, excellent condition, 11-1/2" high, c1870 ($525); Jordan 1-gallon ovoid crock with brush-blue flower and accents at the ear, excellent condition, 9" high, c1850 ($385).

Edmands & Co., 3-gallon preserve jar with dotted triple-flower decoration, 2" tight through-line in front, 6" y-shaped through-line in back and a rim chip on back, 13-1/2" high, c1870 ($210).

From left: E. & L.P. Norton, Bennington, Vt., 1-gallon ovoid crock with slip-plume decoration, through-line in front and spider age-line in back, 9" high, c1870 ($110); 6-quart filter with plume decoration, went on top of larger water cooler, excellent condition, rare form, 8-1/2" high, c1886 ($385).

From left: N. White & Co., Binghamton, N.Y., 4-quart batter pail with blue accents at the spout, ears and at the handle, excellent condition, original tin spout cover and bail handle, 8-1/2" high, c1867 ($415); White & Wood, Binghamton, N.Y., 2-gallon preserve jar with dotted and filled flower, stack-mark in front, glaze discoloration, 11" high, c1885 ($165).

Approximate 3-gallon jar, signed "Eagle Pottery" stenciled inside the banner that is being held by an eagle with spread wings, tight 6" through-line in front and a few minor glaze flecks, 15" high, c1880 ($635).

Unsigned, 3-gallon preserve jar, store mark in blue accent and outline with a double-heart decoration, large base chip with an 8" tight crack up one side, large glued chip in back at rim, unusual piece, 11-1/2" high, c1860 ($305).

Edmands & Co., 2-gallon jar with lid and unusual brush-flower design, separation line and chip at base, minor stone ping, 11-1/2" high, c1870 ($175).

John Burger, Rochester, N.Y., 3-gallon cream pot with large double-flower decoration, glaze burn-spots on side and back in the making, otherwise excellent, 12" high, c1865 ($880).

Edmands & Co., 3-gallon jar with eagle-on-flag decoration, minor stone ping on back and professional restoration to full-length line in front, 13" high, c1870 ($1,870).

Goodwin & Webster, approximate 2-gallon crock with incised bird-and-flower decoration, stone pings, stack-mark and very dark glaze from overfiring, rim chips, 13" high, c1840 ($440).

Unsigned, 4-gallon ovoid crock with flower and bird, attributed to Charlestown, excellent condition, 12-1/2" high, c1840 ($360).

Charlestown, 3-gallon ovoid crock with brush flower and flying bird, 8" tight through-line on one side, some minor lime staining, 11-1/2" high, c1850 ($440).

From left: 1/2-gallon canning jar-stenciled decoration, Parkersburg, W.V., 8" high, c1860 ($80); Geo. W. Miller, Strasburg, Va., 1-1/2-gallon jar with blue-swag decoration, minor chip at base, overall mottled green and brown glaze in the making, 11" high, c1840. The catalog estimate for this piece was $200, but no bid was received.

From left: Unsigned, 2-gallon preserve jar with stylized flower, tight age-line on side, rim chip on back and some overall staining, 11-1/2" high, c1870 ($90); O.L. & A.K. Ballard, Burlington, Vt., 2-gallon preserve jar with light-blue iris decoration, large chip on left ear and surface chips at right ear, 10-1/2" high, c1860 ($90).

Unsigned, 1-gallon pitcher with dotted bird on fence with tree, dark-blue cobalt, probably Edmands, uncommon form and design, very tight age-lines throughout, 10" high, c1870 ($1,020).

N. Clark Jr., Athens, N.Y., 2-gallon cream pot with double-brushed flower decoration, very minor age-line at base and interior rim chip, 9-1/2" high, c1850 ($210).

N.A. White & Son, Utica, N.Y., 5-gallon butter churn with large paddletail bird on flower, 18" high, c1885 ($4,620).

Geddes, N.Y., 6-gallon water cooler with large dotted bird, dated "1860," glaze kiln-burn on side in the making, 15" high, c1860 ($6,050).

Unsigned, 6-quart batter pail with original bale handle and tin spout cap, thick blue flower, excellent condition, 11-1/2" high, c1870 ($550).

Unsigned, approximate 3-gallon pitcher with blue and incised medallion, extensive chips and wear at rim from use, 15" high, c1820 ($210).

From left: Unsigned, 2-gallon pitcher with flower, attributed to Edmands, interior rim chip, 13" high, c1870 ($250); Edmands & Co., 1-gallon jug with dotted bird on flowering branch, professionally restored handle and repair to line in front, 12-1/2" high, c1870 ($250).

From left: Unsigned, 1-gallon batter pail with dotted bow-tie decoration, deep rim chip in back and surface wear at rim and spout, 9" high, c1870 ($250); Whites, Utica, N.Y., 1-gallon cream pot with brushed-flower decoration, over-glaze run on side and back in the making, stone ping in front, 8" high, c1865 ($175).

From left: Burger & Lang, Rochester, N.Y., 1-gallon pitcher with tulip, three chips near flower and 4" line in front, not in the blue, 10" high, c1870 ($305); John Burger, Rochester, N.Y., 2-gallon preserve jar with triple-bud flower in dark-blue slip decoration, very tight through-line on side and rim chip or the back, 10-1/2" high, c1865 ($360).

From left: Lyons, N.Y., 1-gallon preserve jar with brushed-leaf design, minor interior surface chip, 13" high, c1860 ($155); unsigned, 1-gallon pitcher with unusual stenciled and brushed-leaf design, nice form and uncommon design, some staining and light blue in the firing, 10" high, c1860 ($330).

Bristol-glazed water cooler with four polo players in relief design, professional restoration to relief lettering, excellent detail, Whites, Utica, N.Y., 15" high ($770).

From left: Unsigned, 3-quart blind pig with elaborate decoration all over, three-footed base, probably Pennsylvania in origin, some clay discoloration, 7-1/2" high, c1840 ($1,210); unsigned, 1-gallon pitcher with brush-flower decoration and blue accents at the handle, either Pennsylvania or Maryland in origin, 6" very tight line on the back, 10-1/2" high, c1850 ($550).

N.A. White & Son, 5-gallon butter churn with large stylized floral spray, original churn guide, minor 2" tight line over one ear and surface chip at the rim, 17" high, c1885 ($470).

N.A. White & Son, Utica, N.Y., 4-gallon churn with brush- and slip-design, 7" tight line and large rim chip in back and glaze flake spots throughout, 16-1/2" high, c1885 ($90).

Large pedestal-base salt-glaze ice cooler incised, "Bardwell's Root Beer," make-do metal repair to the bottom and one tight 4" line at the rim, great condition for such a large heavy piece of molded pottery, 19-1/2" diameter ($495).

Ottman Brothers & Co., Ft. Edward, N.Y., 4-gallon butter churn with large bird on plume, 8" stabilized crack on back, also through base, some glaze flaking and signs of later over-painting, 17" high, c1875 ($495).

Clark & Fox, Athens, 1-gallon harvest jug, only known signed example ever offered for public sale, very minor touch stack-mark near the name in the making, otherwise excellent 9" high, c1830 ($6,270).

Over the past 25 years, we have received more letters and telephone calls with questions about stoneware than any other single topic. Frankly, we are sick of it and have some questions for you. If you do reasonably well on our queries below, don't call unless it's an emergency. (The answers to the examination are at the end of this section.)

Questions 1 through 5: The following five pieces of Eastern stoneware were sold at the Oct. 6, 1996, mail and telephone auction in Clarence, N.Y. We have provided a picture and description of each of the five. If you were the successful bidder on these five pieces, you would have spent about $8,600 (the price includes a 10% buyer's premium). Based on your extensive knowledge of the stoneware market, match the correct piece with its selling price at auction.

a. $990   b. $165
c. $4,290   d. $2,420
e. $745

____ 1. E. & L.P. Norton, Bennington, Vt., 4-gallon cake crock, 9-1/2" high, two tight lines in front and several surface chips, c1870.

____ 2. J. & E. Norton, Bennington, Vt., 3-gallon jar with crossed peacocks in a tree, 13" high, c1855.

____ 3. Lyons, N.Y., 2-gallon preserve jar, triple-flower decoration, 11-1/2" high, c1860.

____ 4. C.W. Braun, Buffalo, N.Y., 3-gallon crock, eight age-lines, some staining, stone ping, 10-1/2" high, c1860.

____ 5. M. Woodruff, Cortland, N.Y., 3-gallon crock with four-bud flowers, surface chip at the rim, 10-1/2" high, c1860.

8. True or False
This piece dates from the 1830-1840 period.

6. True or False
These pitchers and steins were made in Europe (probably Germany) and have little interest to collectors of America-made stoneware.

9. True or False
A jug with a chicken pecking corn is rarer than a crock with the same decoration.

7. True or False
This decoration was carefully executed with a brush.

10. True or False
This jug dates prior to 1860.

11. True or False
The decoration on this crock was done with a slip-cup.

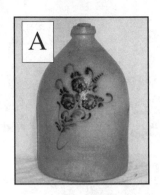

12. True or False
A quick glance from a distance would suggest that the stoneware was probably made in Pennsylvania after 1860.

14. Which piece was decorated with a brush?
A or B?

13. True or False
This churn is worth a minimum of $500.

Mid-Term Examination Answers

1. b	6. False (all are American, most were made in Utica, N.Y.)	10. True
2. c		11. True
3. d		12. False (New York)
4. e	7. False	13. True
5. a	8. False	14. b
	9. True	

CHAPTER 6
INSTANT AUTHORITY: THE SHORT COURSE

This section was developed to provide you with some meaningful information about a cross-section of collecting categories that range from baskets from Massachusetts to molded stoneware from Illinois and Minnesota.

Rustic, Northwoods and Indiana Hickory Furniture

The odds of going to a garage sale or tag sale and finding a 19th century pine cupboard in blue paint are comparable to sharing a Whopper with Elvis in Sarasota, but there is still some hope for a periodic serendipitous experience if you are searching for rustic, Northwoods or Indiana Hickory furniture.

In 1995, we attended a birthday party for a friend at a lodge about 20 minutes from our home in the middle of Illinois. The lodge had been constructed by a local corporation in the 1930s for its employees. When we walked into the large dining hall, we were taken aback to see more than 250 pieces of Old Hickory furniture from Martinsville, Ind., that dated from the 1930s and 1940s which was purchased to furnish the building.

In the past decade, there has been a progressive desire among many "hard core" collectors for something that is good, affordable and available with some effort. Rustic, Indiana Hickory and Northwoods furniture has provided that outlet for many collectors.

Notes on Collecting Rustic and Northwoods

1. Rustic and Northwoods furniture is made of natural materials with the bark left on the wood. The shape of the wood "as found" is incorporated into the design of the piece of furniture.

2. Often, a pine or cedar frame was made and then covered with sheets of peeled birch bark. Twigs, pine cones and even antlers were often added for decoration.

3. Rustic and Northwoods furniture was especially popular and a great deal was made between 1880 and the 1930s. It was constructed from northern Maine to Minnesota. More was created in Wisconsin and Minnesota than in the Adirondack Mountains of New York State.

4. A primary source for rustic and Northwoods furniture is the Adirondack Museum Antiques Show held each year in September in Blue Mountain, N.Y. (Routes 28N and 30). For information, call (518) 861-5062.

Indiana Hickory

1. About a dozen companies in Indiana created a huge assortment of hickory furniture with rattan or splint seats and backs from about 1890 until the 1970s. The Old Hickory Company of Martinsville was the largest and best known. There is still furniture with the Old Hickory impressed-logo being made today.

2. It is possible to date Old Hickory in the following way:

   Prior to 1922: "Old Hickory Chair Co., Martinsville."

   1920s-1930s: "Old Hickory Furniture Co."

   1940s: "Old Hickory, Martinsville, Indiana."

3. In the late 1920s, a small brass circular tag was placed on many of the chairs with two digits that indicated the year of manufacture. Chairs made in 1934 should have "34" in the middle of the brass tag, which is usually found on the inside of a back leg.

4. A primary source for information on Indiana Hickory furniture is Ralph Kylloe's book *A History of the Old Hickory Chair Company and the Indiana Hickory Furniture Movement*. For information, contact Kylloe at P.O. Box 669, Lake George, NY 12845.

Notes on Shaker Rocking Chairs

1. Mt. Lebanon, N.Y., was the center for producing Shaker "production" rocking chairs that were sold to the "world."

2. Initially, the chairs were made for use by the Mt. Lebanon members. Later, they were sold to other Shaker communities and in the immediate area around Mt. Lebanon. The business grew to the point that it eventually offered chairs to department stores and by mail order.

3. In the early 1860s, the chairs were being made in 8 sizes (Nos. O to 7), with the No. 7 being the largest.

4. In the last 25 years of the 19th century, the Seymour Chair Company of Troy, N.Y., made a bentwood rocking chair in the Shaker style that is still being offered at markets and antiques shows as Shaker in origin.

5. In his 1972 *Illustrated Guide to Shaker Furniture*, Robert Meader noted, "The story of both bentwoods and spindle-backs is extremely muddy and confusing and no incontrovertible evidence has come to light to clarify the situation."

6. Collectors should still be exceedingly careful in purchasing any Shaker production rocking chair that differs from the classic form. This would include bentwoods, chairs with "rope" turnings, chestnut examples and spindle-backs. Meader accurately described these forms as "degenerate," when compared to the classic Shaker production rocking chair.

Mid 1870s-early 1880s

- All stretchers are tapered.

Mid 1880s-early 1920s

- The side and rear stretchers are round or cylindrical in form and not tapered.

- The front stretchers are tapered.

Mid 1920s-1942

- All stretchers are cylindrical.

- The back posts of chairs from this period are also straight and not canted or steam "bent," as is the case with earlier chairs.

Five Department Stores that Sold Shaker Chairs in the Late 19th Century

1. Oliver McClintock and Company, Pittsburgh

2. Gayton Furniture Company, Cleveland

3. Troxel Brothers, Burlington, Iowa

4. Marshall Field and Company, Chicago

5. Henry Turner and Company, Boston

SHAKERS'

TRADE   MARK.

MT. LEBANON, N. Y.

The above Trade-Mark will be attached to every genuine Shaker Chair, and none others are of our make, notwithstanding any claims to the contrary.

NOTICE.

All persons are hereby cautioned not to use or counterfeit our Trade-Mark.

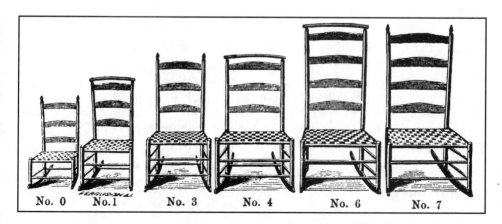

No. 0   No. 1   No. 3   No. 4   No. 6   No. 7

10 Potential Road Trips to See Shaker Collections

1. Smithsonian Institute, Washington D.C.

2. Shaker Museum, Sabbathday Lake, Maine

3. Hancock Shaker Community, Pittsfield, Mass.

4. Greenfield Village, Dearborn, Mich.

5. Canterbury Shaker Village, Canterbury, N.H.

6. Shaker Museum, Old Chatham, N.Y.

7. Golden Lamb Inn, Lebanon, Ohio

8. Warren County Historical Society Museum, Lebanon, Ohio

9. Shelburne Museum, Shelburne, Vt.

10. Shakertown, at Pleasant Hill, Harrodsburg, Ky.

Shaker Rocking Chair Chronology

1789 New Lebanon, N.Y., Shakers make and sell chairs.

1790s The Slossan brothers sell Shaker chairs from a horse-drawn wagon.

1830 The armless "common" chair was priced at $2.50.

1830s Worsted wool tapes or "lists" were first used for seats.

1845 Shaker membership reaches peak of more than 6,000.

1850s A cushion rail is added to some rocking chairs.

1860s The size of the rocking chairs was added for the first time (Nos. 0 to 7).

1870s The Shakers hired outside workers from the "world" to varnish chairs.

1874 A chair catalog was issued for mail-order business.

1875 The gold transfer decal is put on Shaker chairs.

1876 The Shakers receive an award at the Philadelphia Exposition.

1880 E.H. Mahoney of Boston creates a copy of the Shaker rocking chair with "rope" turned parts and markets it.

1885 Enterprise Chair Co., of Oxford, N.Y., offers a spindle-back copy of the Shaker rocking chair.

1900 The Shaker membership rolls drop to less than 1,000 members.

1923 The five-story chair factory at Mt. Lebanon, N.Y., is destroyed by fire on Dec. 28.

1925 L.& G. Stickley Company of Fayetteville, N.Y., offers another copy of the Shaker rocking chair that is constructed of chestnut rather than maple.

1942 The production of rocking chairs is all but over at Mt. Lebanon.

1947 The Mt. Lebanon community closes.

Pie Safes

Perhaps the most difficult piece of country furniture to locate in acceptable and buyable condition is the pie safe. Over the past 30 years, we have seen several thousand pie safes offered for sale; nearly each one has possessed rusted tins, weathered and over-painted surfaces, warped tops and assorted semi-serious to traumatic structural problems. You don't want to own a pie safe that would be better served by the nearest lung machine than in a corner of your living room.

The majority of the safes have also lost some height along the way because they were removed from the house to a wet basement, back porch or leaky-roofed barn where they were used for storage.

Pie safes were common in most rural homes in the second half of the 19th century. Many were constructed of pine and/or poplar and immediately painted. Over time, these safes were periodically updated with a new coat of white, yellow or green paint. Occasionally, pie safes made of cherry or walnut are sometimes discovered with their original unpainted surfaces.

Notes on Collecting Pie Safes

1. The decoration in the hand-punched tins is critical in evaluating a pie safe and can be worth several hundred dollars by themselves. Birds, people, dates and places, Masonic and other lodge logos and animals are known.

2. A painted safe with its original (and not repeatedly over-painted surface) is difficult to find.

3. Factory-made safes have tins that were machine-stamped. If you can, hold up and compare two or more of the tins; if they were machine-stamped, you will note that all the holes line up. The factory safes also tend to be made from a variety of woods.

4. Pie safes with screen wire rather than tins in the doors or on the sides are typically post-1890.

5. The pie safe was a piece of furniture used in a pantry or kitchen to store food and keep insects and rodents from devouring or infesting the family's provisions. Rarely is a safe found without legs a minimum of 8 inches to 12 inches off the floor. It is not a difficult task to add height to safes with problems by "piecing" them out and matching the surface paint.

6. Oak pie safes were factory-made with stamped tins and sold as late as the 1920s.

Shabby Chic

As the amount of country furniture in affordable and acceptable condition continues to diminish and prices escalate, collectors face a dilemma. They must decide if they want to write larger checks, be content with what they already have or look for pieces they would have passed on previously because of a myriad of problems that range from lack of structural integrity to a significantly blemished surface or finish.

Several of the country-related magazines in recent years have featured a look that has come to be called "shabby chic." The eight adjectives most often used to describe pieces of Americana that fall within the definition of shabby chic include:

- Cracked
- Distressed
- Dilapidated
- Worn
- Chipped
- Peeled
- Faded
- Scratched

Our reaction when a shabby chic cupboard appears on the cover of a national magazine is to attempt to understand what the appeal could possibly be to the uninformed collecting public that invest its dollars in it. People could save a lot of money by purchasing a small truck and cruising neighborhoods in their immediate area on the evening before the weekly garbage truck rolls through.

A Windsor chair that has carried its original painted surface through two centuries is timeless it its appearance and will eventually demand respect from generations of collectors not yet conceived.

This is a classic example of shabby chic country furniture. It is the bottom half of a late 19th century pine cupboard that has had its over-painted surface scraped down to leave three distinct coats that remain. The market price currently for this piece would be $350-$500. Ten years ago, it would have been either refinished or had its paint taken down to the base-coat, if it could be saved.

Factory-made kitchen chair, spindle-back, pine seat, maple, over-painted, early 1900s-1920.

On the other hand, a shabby chic kitchen chair with several coats of paint that was manufactured with thousands of others 75 years ago, is timely because it is the look of the moment. As styles and tastes change, the chair will inevitably return to the backroom of the used furniture shop down on the corner where it legitimately belongs.

Notes on Collecting Shabby Chic

If you are going to collect shabby chic Americana, it's important that you understand the following:

1. If the piece you want is not on the top of the pile, drive on down the block, because there will probably be a better one.

2. Merely because you have to lift the piece off the floor to close the door doesn't mean it's been cut down.

3. If you don't like the color of the piece, just scrape it down until you find a color that appeals to you.

4. You can probably assume that somewhere out there is the bottom half of your "hanging cupboard." With luck, you may accidentally cross paths with the guy who thinks he owns a jelly cupboard and put the two together again.

Child's chair, over-painted, maple and pine, early 1900s-1920, probably from an elementary school classroom.

If an article has the patina of age and use, it has value. These cart or buggy wheels would sell for $50-$65 (for the pair).

73

This pine step-back cupboard could be a candidate for the Shabby Chic Hall of Fame. It has: lived a hard life; lost its two bottom doors; misplaced the glass in the upper doors; white paint; the worn exterior that immediately grabs the serious shabby chic fan's eye; minimal value in the real world; a value of about $300-$500 in the surreal world of shabby chic.

It's important that you understand that shabby chic collectors and the readers of the "country look" magazines that feature it, don't care about flaws. They are focused on the moment and what they are told is "hot." This document box is a bit bumped and bruised for our tastes, but it has strong blue paint and just enough wear to excite the serious shabby chic collector. The shabby chic collector would pay $50-$65 for the box.

Molded Stoneware

American stoneware is a product of the 19th century. Mass-produced glassware and the evolution of home refrigeration destroyed the demand for most utilitarian stoneware and closed hundreds of potteries. Those that survived relied on producing specialty pieces and field tile into the 1930s.

Potteries turned to manufacturing a molded product rather than individually-made pieces of stoneware to cut costs and increase output. Each piece was identical and the decoration and maker's mark was quickly applied with a transfer or stencil rather than by an artist with a brush..

Two 10-gallon Lowell Pottery crocks ($100-$135 each).

From left: 3-gallon Monmouth Pottery crock with stenciled maker's name and capacity mark ($75-$115).

2-gallon crock from the Tennessee, Ill., Pottery ($115-$135).

Two "cold drink" coolers from Western Stoneware ($250-$350 each).

2-gallon crock with bristol glaze, c1930s ($425-$55).

6-gallon cooler with bristol glaze and blue sponge decoration ($325-$385).

5-gallon "porch" jug with bristol bottom and Albany slip top, c1930 ($50-$65).

From left: Alexis, Ill., 3-gallon crock ($75-$100); 3-gallon Western Stoneware crock ($75-$95).

2-gallon Western Stoneware crock with bristol glaze ($65-$75).

6-gallon Macomb (Illinois) Stoneware butter churn with stenciled maker's name and capacity mark, c1910 ($150).

Notes on Collecting Molded Midwestern Stoneware of the Early 20th Century

1. Almost all of the Midwestern stoneware made between 1890 and 1930 was molded rather than individually thrown on a potter's wheel.

2. Rarely is a piece of stoneware from this period decorated with other than a stenciled maker's name and capacity mark. Transfers or decals were also popular and quickly applied.

3. A white or bristol glaze was more commonly used than the earlier salt glaze on Midwestern stoneware.

4. The demand for 20th century molded Midwestern stoneware is usually limited to the state or geographic area in which it was made. The Sleepy Eye line of stoneware made at the Monmouth Pottery (Illinois) is an exception and is seriously collected across the United States. Red Wing stoneware from Minnesota also has a national following of collectors.

5. At some point, when the supply of "thrown" cobalt-decorated stoneware is exhausted finally, collectors of the future will turn to early 20th century examples with much more enthusiasm than is shown today.

6. At this point, prices are stagnant and the demand for commonly found pieces of molded Midwestern stoneware is limited.

Nantucket Lightship Baskets

Note: This section was prepared by Americana collectors Steve and Jetsy Sachtleben of Downs, Ill.

The word "Nantucket" means "summer resort" to many people. To others, it's the name of a highly prized basket. These durable baskets were probably first made in the early-to mid 1800s This style of basket, with a wooden bottom and woven rattan sides, is synonymous with Nantucket. The ribs of the basket are inserted into the incised wood bottoms. The exclusive use of molds during the weaving process also is peculiar to Nantucket baskets.

Inside view of basket with 6-1/2" diameter. Note how the wooden ears go down to the wooden base.

From left: Nantucket basket from the last quarter of the 19th century, 8" diameter, wooden ears and desirable brown color, missing some rim lashing cane, slightly out of round ($625); basket from the 1875-1900 period, 6-1/2" diameter, wooden ears, dark-brown patina, beveled base, very minor cane loss ($950).

Lightships or floating lighthouses were used to warn ship captains of danger. They had existed in the United States from about 1820. The first Nantucket lightship was put into service in 1853 and was called the "Nantucket South Shoal." The Nantucket South Shoal crew spent eight months at a time on board the ship and had many free hours between their chores. Basket weaving became a favorite pastime. Molds used during the weaving process were not brought on board until 1856.

Names associated with baskets made on the lightship are Captain Charles Ray, Captain Andrew Sandsbury, William P. Sandsbury, Captain David Ray, Captain Thomas James, Davis Hall, George Swain and W.L. Appleton. By 1905, the Last Nantucketer left the South Shoal Lightship and basket weav-

Oval basket, 6" by 9-1/2", attributed to W.D. Appleton, c1900, finely woven example with brass ears and medium-brown color, handle finely carved, no repairs or cane breakage ($2,000).

Hand-written signature of Mitchell Ray, "Made by Mitchell Ray Nantucket, Mass."

ing on the ship ceased. However, some crew members continued to make baskets on shore and were joined by others who never served on the lightship. A few of the more famous island makers include R. Folger, Mitchell Ray, Ferdinand Sylvaro and, at a later date, Jose Formoso Reyes.

Not all baskets were signed with their maker's name, either by paper label, brand or hand-written signature. Unfortunately, signed examples are found infrequently and demand a high price.

Quality of a Nantucket Lightship Basket

Quality should be measured by what is pleasing to the eye. A desirable basket is well-balanced, in reference to its shape and size of handle. The stave size and their positioning on the basket, the

Interior view of the Appleton basket, showing tight weaving style.

Signed, small oval Nantucket by Mitchell Ray, c1920-45, cruder in workmanship when compared to earlier examples, light-brown color, no breaks or repairs ($1,100).

Round Nantucket basket by William P. Sandsbury. This basket was made on the South Shoal Lightship in the late 19th century. It is in mint condition ($1,750).

rim size and the presence of a well-shaped/turned wooden bottom are all critical.

The best basket bottoms have turned rings and are beveled on the outside. Weaving should be neat, even and tight. The staves must be straight in line from the base to the rim. This gives the basket a pleasing balance and not a "lean" to the right or left. The best baskets have carved handles that are sturdy but, visually, give the basket a feeling of lightness. Color is an important quality to consider in judging a basket. Color is dependent on time and exposure to the environment. An even, rich deep brown is most desirable. Lastly, if the aforementioned qualities are not possessed by a basket, then consider the age and maker of the basket.

A signature on a basket of good quality can greatly increase its value. However, a poor-quality basket regardless of a signature, may be of little value. Generally, the value of a basket is determined by its quality and rarity. Today, common Nantucket baskets may bring $450-$900. Prices escalate as the Nantucket basket quality increases. Single baskets usually are not worth as much as a group of baskets (nest) made by a single weaver as a set. In 1994, a nest of baskets, signed "Davis Hall," sold for $105,000 (plus a buyer's premium) at Sotheby's. They had been part of the "Little Collection." In August 1996, a similar nest sold for "only" $35,000. Also, in August 1996, a nest of seven Captain James baskets sold for $55,000 at Osona's Auction house in Nantucket. Obviously, great fluctuations are apparent in the marketplace, but great Nantucket baskets bring great prices.

Label from the Sandsbury basket with a 7-1/2" diameter: "Made on Board South Shoal Lightship, William P. Sandsbury, Sold by George R. Folger, Main Street, Nantucket, Mass."

If old Nantucket baskets are not within your grasp financially, there are good-quality baskets being made today by contemporary artisans. They will be the antiques of the day after tomorrow. However, when buying a new Nantucket basket, make sure the qualities that make an old one great are manifested in the new one, as well.

Notes on Collecting Nantucket Baskets

1. Round Nantucket baskets are more commonly found than the oval examples.

2. On rare occasions, the baskets are found with the attached paper label

A 7-1/2" round basket with two heart-shaped handles. Attributed to Captain Thomas James of the South Shoals Lightship, c1860-1865, excellent condition, medium-brown color ($2,500).

A round basket with a 11-1/2" diameter by Mitchell Ray. An earlier basket of Ray's, so indicated by its color and quality. The basket is missing some rim-lashing cane, but it is in otherwise good condition. It's best not to replace missing cane as the color differences of the new and old decrease the value of the basket ($700).

of its maker. Some of the names that show up include Jose Formosa Reyes, G.W. Ray, Mitchell Ray and Hall.

3. The "drop" or swing-handled baskets are much more common than baskets with "fixed" handles that do not move.

Interior of the James basket. Some makers used circles on the turned base as their trademarks. Captain James used three sets of circles to indicate his workmanship. The center plug seen on Nantucket basket bases conceals the hole by which the base was secured to the mold.

Paper label of Ray's 11-1/2" basket: "Made by Mitchell Ray, Nantucket, Mass."

4. The baskets originally were called "rattan baskets" and sold to tourists who visited Nantucket.

5. From the standpoint of basket quality, the 1870-1890s period is considered the golden age of Nantucket baskets.

6. The friendship basket (or Nantucket basket purse) dates from just after World War II and were initially made by Jose Formosa Reyes.

7. For more information about Nantucket and its baskets, write to The Nantucket Historical Association, 5 Washington St., Nantucket, MA 02554.

The top of the purse is fitted with an ivory-slotted oval and an ivory dolphin. The dolphin has pieces of its tail and flipper missing.

A woman's purse purchased on Nantucket, c1950. The basket is signed "Anapolis" on the base and had been custom-made, as indicated by the owner's name etched into the ivory inside the lid. Both the latch pin and staple are made of ivory ($2,250).

The hinge portion of the Nantucket purse is even made of ivory, down to the nuts on the inside section. The handle knobs and washers are also of ivory. It is highly unusual to have so much ivory on a Nantucket purse. The purse itself is medium brown in color and has tight weaving.

Contemporary Nantucket basket. The first friendship baskets or purses were made on Nantucket in the years immediately following World War II. This is Becky Warsaw's contemporary purse.

Contemporary Nantucket basket. Among several of the nation's premier contemporary Nantucket basket makers is Becky Warsaw of Colfax, Ill. The tray (at right) is Warsaw's adaptation of the Nantucket form.

CHAPTER 7

ADVERTISING

Advertising—First, a Great Story

On a bitterly cold October Saturday several years ago at an antiques market in Bloomington, Ill., we encountered an elderly man clutching a paper sack tightly in his right hand and uttering a string of profanities that stretched to Peoria. In between curses, he was talking to a mutual friend and relating a story about what was in the sack. The following is a condensed version of his description of what had just occurred to him:

"I always pay the $25 early bird admission to get in here on Saturday and usually find enough to make it worthwhile. Today, it was so cold I decided to take a quick run through the south field to see what the outside dealers had and then go into the buildings. For 32 years, I have collected tobacco tins, and I know what I am looking for. There is a yellow tobacco tin that is in all the books for about $1,500, and that's all I'm going to tell you. For 32 years, I've been trying to find it. So I'm looking through the booths, and I see a yellow tin about the right size and color across the aisle, but I've see hundreds of yellow tins over the years but never the right one.

"I always carry cash, because some dealers prefer it and I can get better prices from them. I had about $1,200 or $1,300, because I never know what I'm going to find. I went over to the booth and picked up the yellow tin and thought I was going to have a [string of expletives deleted] heart attack. It was the one I've been beating the bushes for 32 years. I got so excited that I couldn't get my breath. When I looked at the price tag, it appeared to be $1,295. It was smudged and looked like he had had the piece for awhile by the condition of the tag. I stepped back to gather my thoughts and decided, 'What the hell? I had been looking for more than 30 years, I got the money, I'll buy it.'

"The dealer had another customer, and I stepped back because I was afraid he could hear my heart racing. Finally, he was done and turned to me to see what I wanted. I handed him the tin and said 'What is your best cash price?' He looked at the tag, glanced at me, paused and said, 'I've gotta have $11.'"

Focus of Collectors

The majority of advertising collectors tend to focus on specific categories rather than attempting to purchase and replicate the contents of an entire country store from 1908. These collecting categories may range from unopened rolls of toilet paper to pristine spool cabinets, but the one aspect of advertising memorabilia in which all collectors are in agreement is condition. To have significant value or generate much interest from serious collectors, a piece must be in almost its precise original condition. If it has been reworked, repainted or restored, the value is significantly diminished.

Country furniture collectors can tolerate some minor repairs and isolated cosmetic alternations, and the piece can still keep much of its value; but advertising memorabilia has standards that are much more rigid and unyielding.

In the early 1970s, *The Antique Trader Weekly* carried an advertisement from a firm in Ohio that had discovered a cache of previously uncommon Dan Patch Cut Plug tobacco tins in the depths of an abandoned warehouse. The tins were initially offered for about $10 and were soon found in most antiques shops for the next several years. What had previously been a semi-unusual tobacco tin

immediately lost most of its value because of the Ohio find.

Barns or warehouses filled with pie safes or blue country cupboards just don't happen, because they were handcrafted one at a time and values are much less subject to volatility than advertising. We still see Dan Patch tins for sale 25 years later, and they have gradually climbed to the $50-$75 level.

Dan Patch tin offered for $10 in the early 1970s.

George Washington Cut Plug "lunchbox" tin ($75-$85).

Orcico Cigar tin ($250-$325).

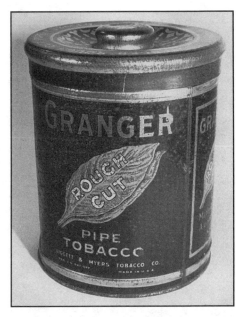

Granger Rough Cut Pipe Tobacco tin ($40-$45).

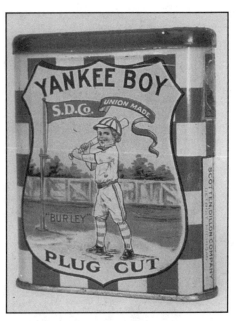

Rare Yankee Boy tin ($700-$800).

Half & Half Lucky Strike tobacco tin ($50-$65).

Kildow's Panetela tin ($75-$95).

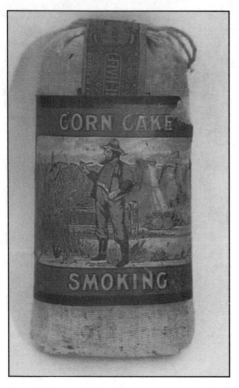

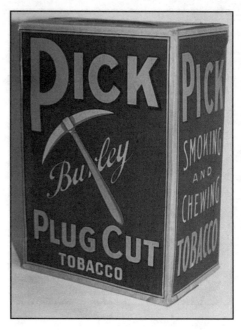

Oversized box of Pick Plug Cut tobacco ($175-$200).

Pouch of Corn Cake Smoking tobacco ($50-$70).

New Bachelor 5-cent cigar box ($100-$120).

Winnie Winkle cigar box ($100-$120).

Indian Ax cigar box ($85-$100).

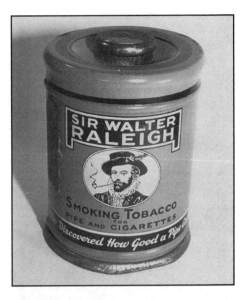

Sir Walter Raleigh smoking tobacco tin ($30-$45).

Rock-Co 2-pound cocoa tin ($60-$75).

Baby Stuart Cocoa tin, 1 pound ($60-$75).

Lowney's Cocoa tin, 1/2 pound ($60-$75).

None-Such Cocoa tin, 1 pound ($60-$75).

Elkay Cocoa tin, 1 pound ($30-$40).

Monarch Cocoa tin, 1 pound ($35-$50).

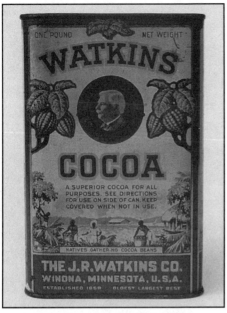

Watkins Cocoa tin, 1 pound ($45-$60).

Index Brand Coca tin, 1 pound ($150-$175).

Our Mother's Cocoa tin, 2 pounds ($35-$50).

Golden Rule Cocoa tin, 5 pounds ($60-$75).

Monarch Tea tin ($35-$50).

Yum Yum Smoking Tobacco tin ($175-$200).

College Maid cigar box ($50-$65).

Old Rip tobacco tin ($275-$300).

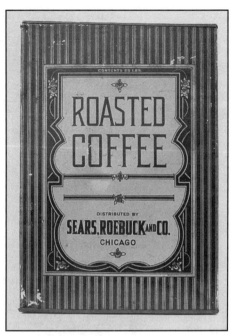

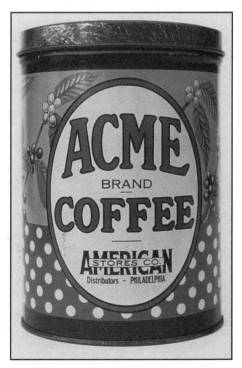

Sears-Roebuck & Co. Coffee tin, 10 pounds ($150-$175).

Sears-Roebuck & Co., Coffee bin, 25 pounds ($250-$275).

Chocolate Cream Coffee tin, 3 pounds ($150-$175)

Acme Coffee tin, 1 pound ($65-$85).

Old Master Coffee tin, 1 pound ($75-$90).

Your Luck Coffee tin, 2 pounds ($75-$90).

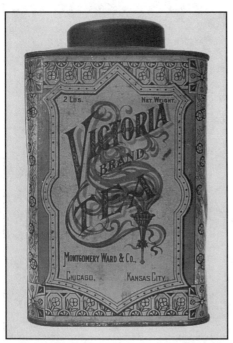

Victoria Brand 2-pound tea tin ($60-$75).

Variety of cocoa tins ($50-$100 each).

1-pound coffee tins ($75-$125 each).

Richelieu Roasted Coffee tin, 3-pound size ($100-$125).

Rare Ferndell coffee grinder with wall mount ($325-$375).

Walter Baker & Co. cocoa box ($55-$65).

Queen's Taste coffee tin ($65-$75).

Old Time Blended Coffee tin ($95-$115).

Breakfast Call Coffee tin ($75-$85).

Advo Gold Medal Coffee tin ($75-$90).

Elgin grocery store coffee grinder, re-placed eagle finial ($600-$800).

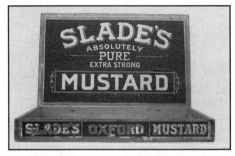

Slade's Mustard box, paper labels ($225-$275).

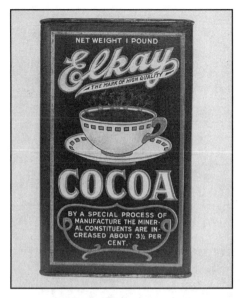

Fairbank's Fairy Christmas Soap box, 17" by 16" ($350-$500).

Fairbank's Fairy Soap box, 1896, 17" by 16" ($300-$375).

Maple Gove Soap box ($135-$150).

Prima Donna Soap box ($250-$275).

Oak J. & P. Coats spool chest ($600-$800).

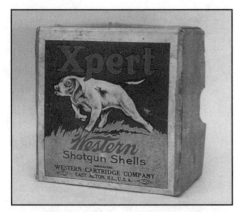

Xpert Western shotgun shells box ($125-$150).

Pointer shot-gun shells box ($125-$150).

Old Label baking powder tin ($20-$25).

Calumet Baking Powder tin ($12-$16).

Egg-O Baking Powder tin ($20-$25).

Stone fruit, early 1900s **($45-$65 each).**

Tin coffee bin, c1900 **($375-$425).**

Buttocks basket **($225-$275).**

Sibley seed box **($400-$500).**

Blue pie safe, early 1900s
($900-$1,200).

Rustic plant stand **($135-$150).**

Pine step-back cupboard **($3,000-$4,000).**

Painted basket **($300-$365).**

Apple-green pie safe **($1,200-$1,600**

Splint wash basket **($300-$335).**

Weathervane horses **($200-$250 each).**

Snow shoes **($125-$140).**

Bushel basket **($50-$75).**

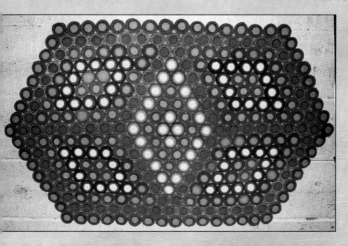

Penny rug **($300-$375).**

Basket collection (**$200-$1,200**).

Running-horse weathervane (**$600-$950**).

"Chalk" cat, c1920 (**$65-$75**)

Canoe paddles
(**$50-$75 each**).

*Painted
candlemold*
(**$200-$240**).

Gas eagle from 1920s
filling station
($1,000-$1,500)

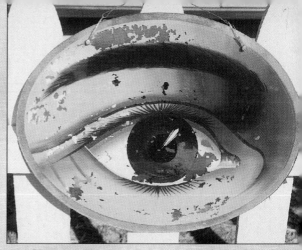

Glass eye from optician's sign **($135-$175)**.

"Chalk" compote
($200-$240).

Arrow-back
side chair
($175-$200).

Straw-filled Santa Claus
figure **($300-$350)**.

Fabric pin cushions **($65-$85 each).**

Rare tin spice box **($400-$500).**

Pantry boxes in blue paint **($1,600-$1,800 for stack of four).**

"Memory" jug **($300-$350).**

Rabbit door-stop **($400-$500).**

Doll dressed as a
baseball player,
early 1900s
($1,500-$1,800).

Jelly cupboard ($1,000-$1,300).

Three Shaker berry buckets
($1,200-$1,500 all three).

Toy doll and dog ($650).

Toy train ($275-$325).

Painted table **($300-$375).**

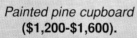

Painted pine cupboard
($1,200-$1,600).

Painted cupboard **($450-$525).**

"Mogul" windmill weight
($2,000-$2,500).

Molded stoneware, early 1900s
($400-$550 each).

Mirex Quality First cigar tin ($45-$55).

Lemon Wafers tin, 14 oz. ($20-$25).

Texie cigar box ($150-$165).

Badger Matches container ($15-$20).

New Rival shotgun shell box ($65-$75).

VanDerveer & Holmes Biscuit Company crate with paper labels ($125-$150).

Roast Mutton tin ($25-$35).

Armour's Calf Brains in 5-pound container ($25-$30).

Krak-R-Jak Biscuits tin ($75-$95).

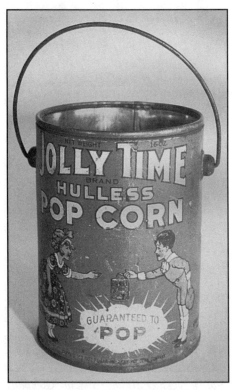

Jolly Time Pop Corn tin ($15-$20).

Bar of Big Jack laundry soap and Blue Barrel laundry soap ($9-$12 each).

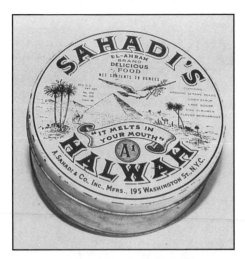

Sahadi's Halwah food tin ($25-$30).

Beaver Brand hat box ($20-$25).

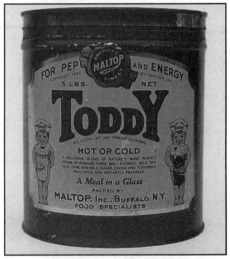

Toddy Beverage tin, 5 pound ($100-$125).

Rare Heinz Apple butter crock with paper label ($300-$400).

Star Maid Salted Peanuts tin, 10 pounds ($225-$250).

Rawleigh's Black Pepper tin, 1 pound ($30-$35).

Blossom Sweet Honey tin, 5 pounds ($25-$30).

ReJoyce Pepper tin ($75-$85).

Queen Cocoanut tin ($75-$100).

Dunham's Cocoanut tin ($150-$175).

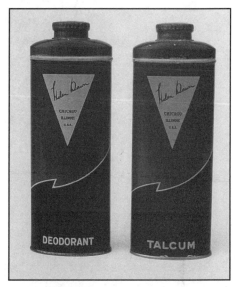

Helen Dawn Deodorant and Talcum tins ($35 each).

Golden Hey Baking Powder, 1 pound ($35-$40).

Lanco Brand Rolled Oats box ($65-$80).

Purity Brand Rolled Oats box ($65-$80).

White Villa Brand Rolled Oats box ($90-$100).

Purity Fruit Cake tin ($25-$30).

Betty Brown's California Fruit Cake tin ($20-$25).

Brioschi & Co., medicine bottle ($25-$35).

DeLoney's Hair Scalp Tonic bottle ($30-$35).

Health-O Lilac After Shave ($25-$35).

Viz Herb Remedy bottle ($25-$35).

Maltine Medicine bottle ($25-$35).

Rollins Childrens' stocking advertisement ($75-$85).

Argo Corn Starch box, 1 pound ($30-$35).

Parrot Food box, Huth Seed Company ($16-$20).

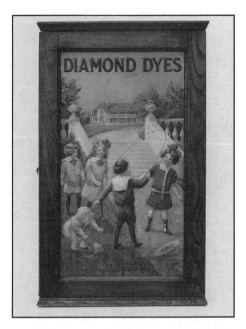

Diamond Dyes oak display case ($650-$1,000).

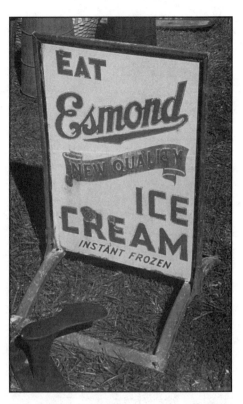

Eat Edmond Ice Cream sidewalk sign ($135-$150).

Boye Needle Company display case for needles ($325-$375).

Queen Soda Cracker tin ($60-$75).

Prairie Brand Cracker Crate ($35-$50).

Pennzoil storage rack and eight cans ($300-$350).

P.O.C. Beer sign ($90-$120).

Texaco key holder for restroom and keys ($85-$100).

Mobiloil Gargoyle rack with 12 cans ($1,000-$1,300).

Flower & Vegetable Seed Boxes

A decade ago, many Americana dealers were unfamiliar with seed boxes when a collector inquired about them. Seed boxes are now enjoying greater exposure, and dealers are much more familiar with this collectible. The increased interest in seed boxes can be observed by the number of people bidding on them at auction as well as the prices collectors are willing to pay for them. In fact, some auctioneers now highlight seed boxes in their auctions.

There seems to be an endless variety of seed box styles and graphics, but it is easiest to group them into three main categories. These would include flower seed boxes, vegetable seed boxes and Shaker seed boxes.

Flower Seed Boxes

Flower seed boxes are the most common seed boxes found and generally date from around the turn of the century. They are typically made of oak with dove-tailed sides. They are commonly approximately 12" by 7". Unlike any of the other boxes, flower boxes often have only an inside label. Many seed companies marketed flower seeds more creatively with labels depicting children, animals and beautiful gardens. To further display the flower seeds, some companies displayed their product in inlaid wooden boxes with decorative hardware. Many of these flower seed boxes were saved by later generations because of the decorations. D.M. Ferry, Rice's and Mandeville & King and Company made numerous labels and are the three most frequently found boxes by collectors today.

Vegetable Seed Boxes

Vegetable seed boxes are generally larger than flower seed boxes and are typically 21" by 10". Vegetable seed boxes are usually made of pine and have several inside dividers with both inside and outside labels. The inside labels typically have lovely pictures of vegetables, while the outside labels are more simple. These boxes are much more difficult to locate than the flower seed boxes, especially in good condition. Many of the vegetable seed boxes were used to store tools and ended up in barns and garages and are more often found in rougher condition.

To bring top dollar today, the boxes should have both inside and outside labels in very good condition with exceptional graphics. Intact original dividers add more value. These boxes are very hard to find in today's market. Most of the boxes uncovered today have outside labels in fair to poor condition, but if the box has a beautiful inside label in very good condition, today's collector cannot afford to pass them up, as long as they are within the ballpark of affordability.

Shaker Seed Boxes

Shaker seed boxes are in a class by themselves. All Shaker seed boxes are products of the 19th century. The Shaker seed industry lost its luster by the last quarter of the 19th century; its business began to fade and the boxes disappeared.

Shaker seed boxes are very difficult to locate. The inside labels are almost always missing, so the outside label most often determines the value. The outside labels typically have tears or parts of the label missing, fading or major stains, and they will still have a high price tag. Shaker seed boxes are frequently sought out and therefore command a higher price from collectors.

Because of the limited number of quality seed boxes offered for sale, there has been a wide variance in pricing. Keep in mind for a seed boxes to command high prices, the box should have all labels in good condition with attractive graphics. As collectors and dealers become more familiar with seed boxes, pricing will, hopefully, become more stable.

Many of the seed boxes illustrated in this section are from the extensive collection of Todd and Marlene Harting. The Hartings are serious collectors of seed boxes and seed-industry collectibles. Individuals with seed boxes for sale or with questions can contact the Hartings at 19515 Manchester Ct., Mokena, IL 60448 (708) 479-1749.

Notes on Collecting Shaker Seed Boxes

1. The most commonly found boxes are products of the Mount Lebanon, N.Y., community.

2. The New Lebanon, N.Y., seed boxes pre-date 1861.

3. The typical seed box was constructed of pine, nailed together, painted or stained a deep red, had a rectangular paper label on the front of the box and an interior label that listed the variety of seeds it held. The hinges were made of leather and tacked to the top of the box or a variation of the cotter pin.

4. It is extremely difficult in today's market to find a box with both interior and exterior paper labels. Typically, the interior label has been peeled off or badly ripped and the exterior label has some damage.

5. Condition is relative with Shaker seed boxes. Labels become brittle over time and chip away. When the boxes were returned to the Shakers each fall from the store keepers, they were repainted or repaired and new labels were often glued over last year's variety. In the spring, the refurbished boxes once again were returned to the stores filled with packets of seeds.

6. Shaker seed boxes are occasionally found with pristine exterior labels that suggest they may have been added to an old box from a pile of newly discovered labels that were never used.

Significant Dates in the History of the Shaker Seed Industry

1790s Seeds were being sold in Watervliet, N.Y., and New Lebanon, N.Y.

1794 Garden seed industry begins on a larger scale at New Lebanon

1870s A gradual decline in demand for Shaker-grown seeds, due to increasing competition from national companies, creates problems for the Shaker seed industry.

1890s The Mt. Lebanon Shakers close their seed industry, due to falling membership and a lack of workers.

D.M. Ferry & Co., flower seed box, 12" by 7", 1893, inlaid walnut lid, excellent graphics by J. Ottman Company ($200-$225).

D.M. Ferry & Co., flower seed box, oak, 11-1/2" by 7" ($125-$150).

D.M. Ferry & Co., flower seed box, oak, 11-1/2" by 7" ($150-$175).

Briggs Bros., flower seed box, 10" by 7" ($125-$150).

S.F. Leonard flower seed box, 10" by 7" ($125-$150).

Rice's flower seed box, inlaid walnut lid, excellent graphics by J. Ottman Company, 11" by 6-1/2" ($200-$225).

Jesse Lines Seed Co., flower seed box, oak, 8" by 6" ($90-$100).

D.M. Ferry flower seed box, pine, 7" by 4", early flower seed box with rare outside label ($250-$300).

N.J. Burt & Co., flower seed box, 8" by 6" ($60-$75).

Rice's flower seed box, small oak, 6" by 5" ($100-$125).

Rice's flower seed box, inlaid wood sides and lid, 6" by 5", graphics by J. Ottman Company ($125-$150).

D.M. Ferry & Co., flower seed box, oak, 1906, most commonly found, available in several sizes, 11-1/2" by 6-1/2", with outside label ($75-$90); without outside label ($50-$65).

Rice's flower seed box, carved oak, 11" by 7" ($150-$175). There are several variations of the House & Garden series.

Mandeville & King Co., flower seed box, oak, 11-1/2" by 4-1/2", most commonly found Mandeville & King box, available in several sizes ($50-$65).

Rice's flower seed box, cardboard, 10" by 3" ($50-$65).

Mandeville & King Co., flower seed box, cardboard, 11" by 8" ($50-$65).

M.G. Madson Seed Co., flower seed box, walnut, 11-1/2" by 5" ($90-$100).

D.M. Ferry & Co., seed box, pine, 9" by 6" ($50-$65).

*L.L. May & Company seed box, pine, 21"
by 10" ($275-$300).*

*Manitowoc Seed Co., flower seed box, un-
usual metal box, 9" by 6" ($50-$65).*

*D.M. Ferry & Co., flower seed box, oak, 9-
1/2" by 7" ($125-$150).*

*D.M. Ferry & Co., flower seed box, 12" by
7", inlaid walnut lid, excellent graphics by
J. Ottman Company ($200-$225). Also
made in larger size of about 16" by 8".*

*Rice's flower seed box, oak, 11" by 9"
($150-$175).*

*Rice's Flower Seed box, oak, 11" by 6-1/2"
($150-$175).*

Ferry's seed box, 24" by 11", outside label with small inside label describing display set-up of metal tray inserts ($125-$150).

Rush Park Seed Co., pine, 21" by 10", inside label in excellent condition with worn outside label ($275-$300).

Sioux City Nursery & Seed Company, vegetable seed box, pine, 25" by 13" ($325-$350).

Rush Park Seed Co., vegetable seed box, pine, 27" by 13", inside label in excellent condition ($225-$250).

Jesse Lines Seed Co., seed box, rare early pine box, simple black-and-white graphics, 12" by 12" ($100-$125).

Briggs Brothers & Company, vegetable seed box, pine, 24" by 10" ($275-$300).

From left: Lyman's seed box, pine, 21" by 9", nice example of an outside label, though inside label is plain ($200-$225); Rice's seed box, pine, 24" by 10", missing inside label ($150-$175).

Shaker seed box, New Lebanon, N.Y., mid-1850s 14-1/2" by 7" ($1,300-$1,500).

Lone Star Seed Co., seed box, no inside label ($75-$100).

Page's display seed box, oak, 24" by 17" ($325-$350).

Ross Brothers Company display seed box with wooden trays, red-painted pine, 25" by 12" ($275-$300).

D.M. Ferry & Company, seed shipping crate, green-painted pine, 30" by 18" ($325-$350).

Mel Webster Seedsman, vegetable seed box, pine, 30" by 14", nice colorful inside label with original dividers, outside label missing ($225-$250).

Shaker seed box, Mt. Lebanon, N.Y., c1870s, 23-1/2" by 11-1/2" ($1,200-$1,500).

Shaker seed box, Mt. Lebanon, N.Y., c1880s, 23-1/2" by 11-1/2" ($1,400-$1,600).

Shaker seed box, Mt. Lebanon, N.Y., mid-1880s, 22" by 11", odd box usually found without a lid, lid replaced on box illustrated ($1,400-$1,600).

Rice's seed crate for mailing packs to stores, 21" by 7" ($100-$125).

D.M. Ferry flower seed box, oak, early 20th century ($100-$125).

Mandeville & King's flower seed box, 12" by 8-1/2" ($100-$125).

Mandeville & King flower seed box, 12" by 8-1/2" ($100-$125).

Mandeville & King flower seed box, 12" by 8-1/2" ($85-$100).

Huth Seed Company, San Antonio, seed packets ($4-$5 each).

Burpee's seed crate ($60-$70).

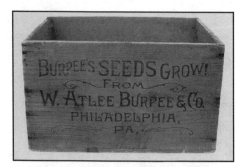

Jesse Lines Seed Company, seed packets with original contents ($10-$12 each).

Miss C.H. Lippincott Flower Seed Catalog, 1895 ($30-$35).

Rice's flower seed box, 11" by 9" ($150-$175).

Gurney Seed & Nursery Company, catalogs, early 1920s ($20-$25 each).

Wayne Seed Company seed packs ($3-$4 each).

Burt seed packs ($3-$4 each).

Card seed packs ($3-$4 each).

Shaker seed packets from Canterbury, N.H. ($75-$90 each).

Mt. Lebanon, N.Y., Shaker seed packet ($100-$125).

West Pittsfield, Mass., Shaker seed packet ($100-$125).

New Lebanon, N.Y., Shaker seed packet ($100-$125).

CHAPTER 8
SHOPS, MARKETS & AUCTION HOUSES

AMERICAN ROOTS

A unique collection of early American country antiques can be found at American Roots, a multi-group shop located in the downtown historic district of Orange, Calif. American Roots specializes in original and early painted furniture, vintage textiles, decorated stoneware, toys and folk art. American Roots can be contacted at: 105 W. Chapman Ave., Orange, CA 92666, (714) 639-3424. The shop is open 10 a.m. to 5 p.m. Monday through Saturday and from noon to 5 p.m. on Sunday.

Q&A with Dealer/Collector Manuela Yokota

Manuela Yokota is a collector/Americana dealer in southern California who has merchandise for sale at American Roots in Orange, Calif.

Q. What is the state of the country and Americana antiques market in California?

A. Considering the state of the economy in California, the country and Americana antiques market is holding up pretty well.

Q. Are there any specific items or categories that collectors are seeking?

A. Woodenware, textiles, samplers, toys and holiday-related items—the higher the quality, the better.

Q. Do you feel that the interest and demand for Americana is growing?

A. The more Americans relate to their heritage, the more interest for Americana.

Q. Is there much of a market for painted furniture?

A. Yes, there is, and it is increasing each year. .

Q. Have you found some items in California that you haven't seen or been offered anywhere else?

A. You can often find good-quality Americana at a better price than back East.

Q. Are there any country-oriented shows that you recommend?

A. Simply Country (Washington). California Country (Los Altos, Calif.)

"Cat" hooked rug in excellent condition, c1900 ($350).

Early ticking pillows filled with feathers ($45-$95 each).

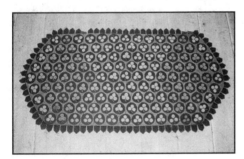

Unusual penny rug ($295).

Black horse hooked rug, c1910-20s ($950).

Hooked rug with a winter village scene ($285).

Fabric-art doll wearing a red dress, c1900 ($275).

Hooked rug with a beaver ($325).

From left: Light blue piggin with iron bands ($295); mustard-painted wall box ($275).

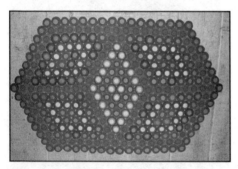

Child's rocking horse on pine frame and rockers, early 1900s ($475-$600).

Very colorful penny rug, c1920 ($295).

Early 1900s child's rocking horse, missing its base and rockers, hide and original saddle and bridle ($675-$850).

Fredonia, N.Y., seed rack with empty seed packets, c1920s ($200).

Two bisque Jack-O-Lanterns with character faces, made in Germany, unusual, almost 4" tall ($195 each).

Blue-painted bucket bench, boot-jack ends, found in Massachusetts ($465).

From left: Red and black grain-painted bucket ($135); blue-covered bucket ($195); red keeler with iron bands, on top ($195).

Screen-wire pie cupboard in pumpkin paint, c1900 ($850).

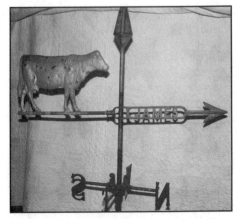

Early 20th century weathervane, made by James ($325).

From left: Early litho doll, dated 1901 ($295); pin cushion ($25).

Small mustard-painted storage cupboard, pine, early 1900s ($295).

From left: Early child's wash bench in blue paint ($295); child's two-drawer chest in mustard paint ($195).

From left: Blue-and-white spongeware fluted bowl ($155); pitcher ($225); advertising pitcher ($65); spittoon ($135).

Architectural cupboard from a house in Maine, painted pine, c1820 ($995).

Pennsylvania apothecary chest of eight drawers in blue paint, c1900 ($895).

Brown, red and white game board, pine, early 1900s ($275).

Red, white and blue folk-art house, c1920s ($525).

From left: German die-cut Jack-O-Lantern witch ($125); cardboard skeleton of witch, 1930s ($22); 15" Georgene Raggedy Ann ($125); 19" Georgene Raggedy Ann ($150); 1920s party hats ($20 each).

Waldoborough-style hooked rug in dark browns and reds, c1900 ($295).

From left: Three bisque dolls ($45, $385, $120).

A. GRIDLEY ANTIQUES

A. Gridley Antiques is a large general-line shop in downtown Bloomington, Ill., that is reminiscent of the antiques emporiums of 30 years ago. The shop carries a wide variety of furniture, ranging from country to Victorian; it also carries textiles, glass, advertising and folk art. The shop is open on Wednesday and Thursday by chance and is open from 11 a.m. to 5 p.m. on Friday and Saturday. For more information, contact A. Gridley Antiques, 217-219 E. Front St., Bloomington, Il. 61702, (309) 829-9615.

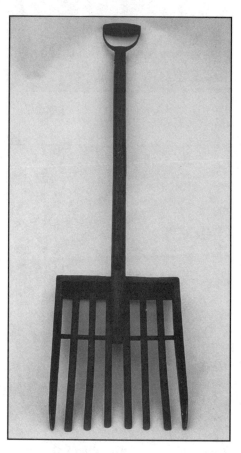

Factory-made fruit scoop, early 20th century ($100-$125).

Turned-maple food masher, early 20th century ($25-$30).

Factory-made knife and fork box, maple, original natural finish, late 19th century ($100-$125).

Painted pine utility box, nailed together, early 20th century ($50-$60).

Homemade knife and fork box, painted pine, nailed sides, early 20th century ($65-$75).

Maple grain scoop, 34" tall, one piece of maple, c1900 ($200-$240).

Pine knife and fork box, homemade, natural finish ($50-$60).

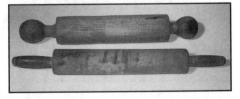

Tool box, painted pine, nailed sides, early 1900s ($75-$95).

Turned-maple rolling pins, factory-made, early 1900s ($45-$50 each).

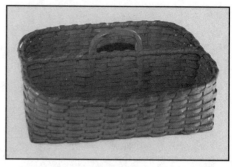

Knife and fork basket, painted green ($200-$225).

Oak-splint half basket, rib construction ($135-$150).

Pantry box with drop-handle, factory-made, painted finish, late 19th/early 20th century ($175-$200).

Coffee mill, early 20th century ($100-$120).

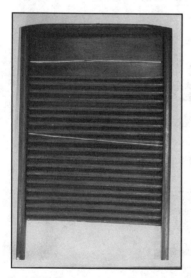

Washboard, factory-made, walnut, c1900 ($135-$150).

Shaker cheese box, painted yellow maple and pine, New England, late 19th century ($650-$750).

Indiana hickory chair, original condition, c1930s ($200-$250).

Rustic table, original condition, c1930 ($50-$65).

Oversized bird house with original dome, probably a later repaint, 38" diameter, c1940 ($175-$250).

Set of four factory-made half-spindle chairs, original painted finish, c1880 ($475-$575).

Oak wall telephone, working condition, original finish, c1930s ($275-$325).

Bristle brush with red-painted and turned-maple handle, early 20th century ($65-$75).

6-gallon molded crock, Bristol glaze, Western Stoneware, 1920 ($65-$75).

Shaker duster with original ribbon, sold in tourist or gift shops at Shaker New England communities, turned-maple, c1900 ($150-$185).

Molded "porch" jug, 5-gallon with Albany slip-top ($75-$100).

Shaker clothes brush with blue velvet cover, turned-maple handle, New England, early 1900s ($95-$120).

Close-up view of "Memory" jug.

"Memory" jug, decorated with items from someone's childhood, made during early 20th century craft revival using molded stoneware jug ($300-$350).

Brush-decorated ovoid jug from 1830-40 period, no maker's mark ($225-$250).

Rare six-drawer spice chest, factory-made, mid 19th century ($325-$425).

Tin spice chest, factory-made, original painted and lettered surface, late 19th/early 20th century ($300-$400).

Factory-made spice chest, original pulls and surface, early 1900s ($225-$275).

"Chalk" cat, original painted surface, minor chips, c1930 ($85-$125). Though usually labeled as "chalk," cats of this period are made of Plaster of Paris rather than chalk.

Factory-made wooden spice box, original stenciled lettering, early 20th century ($200-$225).

Rare black cat of molded cardboard, original paper liner, c1940s ($125-$150).

Jack-O-Lantern of molded cardboard, original paper liner, c1940s ($95-$115).

Jack-O-Lantern, c1940s ($95-$115).

Unusual expression on face of 1940s Jack-O-Lantern ($75-$95).

Jack-O-Lantern with original paper liner, c1940s ($125-$150).

Easter rabbit made from pressed cardboard, similar to the Jack-O-Lanterns, c1940s ($65-$75).

Devil, fairly rare form with original paper liner, c1940s ($150-$200).

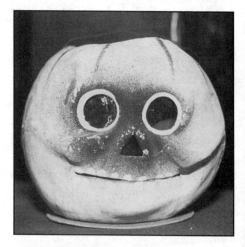

Rare skeleton, c1930s ($225-$250).

Majolica floral creamer ($75-$100).

Santa Claus filled with straw, 19" tall, original condition, "mask" face, c1930s ($300-$335).

Etruscan majolica sunflower pitcher ($375-$425).

Etruscan majolica, Griffin, Smith & Hill, butterfly-lip creamer ($200-$225).

Cast-iron snow eagle, late 1800s ($75-$95).

Cast-iron snow eagle, applied to roof to hold snow, late 19th century ($95-$125).

Cast-iron dog nutcracker, c1900 ($60-$75).

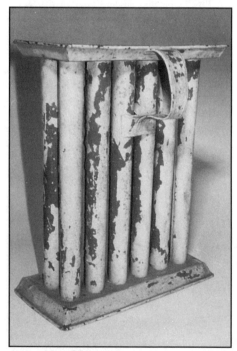

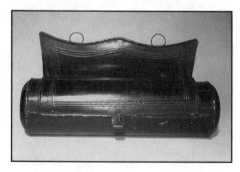

Painted tin candlebox, 19th century, factory-made ($275-$300).

Twelve-tube tin candlemold, painted finish, late 19th century ($200-$240).

Child's lunch box, painted blue, factory-made, early 1900s ($45-$55).

Rare star governor weight, cast iron, Kendallville, Ind., c1915 ($450-$600).

Cast-iron iron, late 19th century ($30-$40).

Cast-iron muffin pan, early 1900s ($55-$65).

Cast-iron match holder, early 1900s ($35-$45).

Cast-iron kettle, early 1900s ($65-$80).

Cast-iron pot with drop-handle ($45-$55).

Miniature cast-iron kettle, c1900 ($100-$135).

Factory-made ice tongs, c1920s ($20-$30).

Tin pail for taking liquid refreshment to school or work with a packed lunch, late 19th century ($30-$35).

Early 20th century dog nutcracker, original finish ($60-$75).

Cast-iron and brass scale with weights ($50-$75).

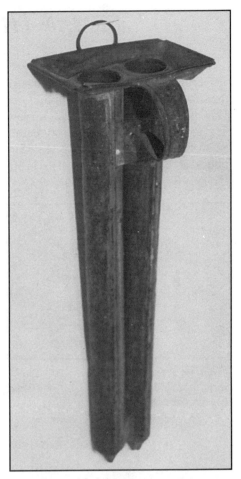

Two-tube tin candlemold, late 19th century ($150-$200).

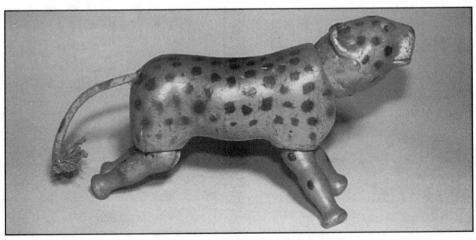

Schoenhut tiger, "reduced size," painted eyes, c1930s ($375-$400).

GERMAN HILL ANTIQUES

German Hill Antiques is located near the small Central Illinois community of Downs. German Hill specializes in New England antiques with original or painted surfaces. Contact German Hill Antiques at Box 42, Downs, IL 61736, (309) 378-4350.

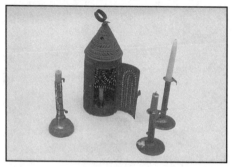

From left: Punched-tin lantern ($200-$300); spiral candlestick ($300-$400); two signed hogscraper candlesticks ($175 each).

Bannister-back armchair, New Hampshire, red and black graining, mid 18th century ($2,500-$3,000).

Sheraton Windsor side chair, yellow with painted decoration, c1820 ($750-$800).

Arrowback Windsor double-rocker, grain-painted to look like oak, c1830 ($900-$1,000).

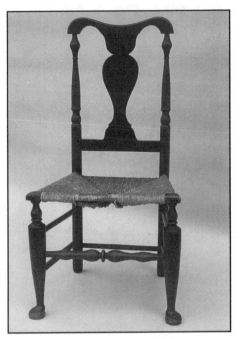

Hudson River Valley side chair with duck feet, old refinish, mid 18th century ($1,200-$1,300).

New England fan-back Windsor side chair, signed, original black paint, late 1700s ($1,800-$2,000).

New England Windsor armchair, black paint, probably Rhode Island in origin, 18th century ($3,500-$4,200).

Extremely rare Windsor foot stool, original finish, 18th century ($2,500-$2,750).

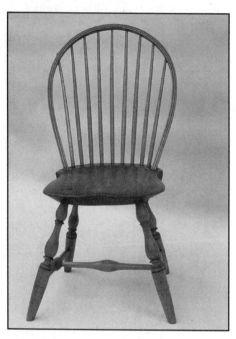

Refinished bulbous-turned Windsor side chair, New England, 18th century ($1,000-$1,600).

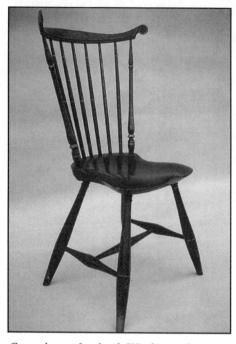

Carved ear, fan-back Windsor side chair, Rhode Island, original black paint with later gilt decoration ($3,000-$3,500).

Ladder-back armchair, New Jersey, old black over original orange paint, 18th century ($2,250-$2,600).

Bannister-back side chair, scraped to original green paint, original seat, mid 18th century ($1,200-$1,500).

Connecticut sack back Windsor, black over red paint, late 18th century ($3,200-$3,700).

Queen Anne curly maple drop-front desk, traces of red paint, 18th century ($4,000-$5,000).

Lancaster County, Pennsylvania, dough box on legs with drawer, original brown paint over red wash ($3,000-$3,200).

Child's settee bench, Western Massachusetts, old refinish, lift-up seat, 18th century ($2,500-$3,000).

New England pine server, bracket base, dovetailed gallery, original blue-gray paint, c1820-40 ($1,750-$2,250).

One-drawer taper-legged stand, original red paint on base, traces of putty paint on top, original pull, c1825-45 ($1,200-$1,500).

From top: Stack of firkins—mustard ($450); red ($325); sage green ($425).

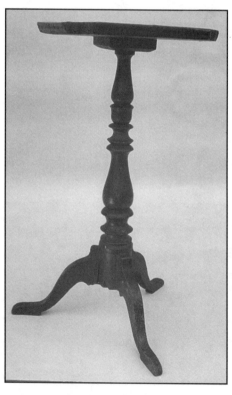

Snake-foot candlestand, red and green paint, New England, 18th century ($2,000-$2,200).

Schoenhut ringmaster, bisque head, original clothes, early 1900s ($400-$500).

Portrait of young boy in a blue dress holding a book, found in Vermont estate, c1840 ($7,500-$10,000).

L. Norton, Bennington, Vt., 4-gallon ovoid jar with blue flower ($700-$800).

L. Seymour, Troy, N.Y., 2-gallon ovoid jar, blue flower ($400-$500).

AMERICAN HARVEST ANTIQUES

American Harvest Antiques is a four-dealer group of shops that specializes in early country furniture and accessories with their original paint or surface. The business is located in the historic Ohio River community of Paducah, Ky., and can be reached by taking Exit 4 off of Interstate 24 and proceeding east about 5 miles before turning left onto North 6th Street. The shop is in a century-old building at the corner of North 6th and Park Avenue. American Harvest is open on Wednesdays from 10 a.m. to 5 p.m., and Saturdays from 10 a.m. to 4 p.m. To reach the shop, call (502) 442-4852.

48-drawer cabinet, found in Illinois, old cream paint ($350-$450).

Three painted candleboxes, 19th century ($250-$350 each).

Folky four-drawer spice cabinet, original painted surface ($300-$350).

Early rocking horse from Tennessee, 19th century ($875-$1,100).

Coffee pot, stoneware with Albany slip, pewter lid and handle, brass bottom ($145).

Corner cupboard from a log cabin in Indiana, pegged and mortised, cream over red-painted surface ($2,000-$2,800).

Crudely executed, early log cabin, probably a toy for a child ($100-$125).

Pipe box with heart and leather hinges ($200-$250).

Early pine box, heart and folk-art carvings, pumpkin paint ($250).

Folky 16-tin weeping willow pie safe, found in Kentucky, turned legs, refinished ($4,000-$5,000).

Mustard-painted corner cupboard, pine-scalloped shelves, c1830 ($3,500-$4,000).

Red-painted step-back cupboard, maple, raised panels inside, shelf grooves for plates, spoon rack, c1820 ($3,500-$4,000).

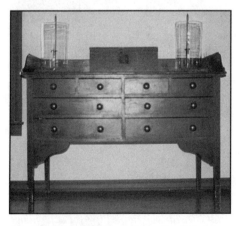

Grain-painted server, pine, splash-back, eight drawers, c1850 ($3,000-$3,500).

From left: Blue-painted cant-back shelf, pine, c1850 ($300-$375); sewer-tile spariel ($125-$175).

Red desk-on-frame, pine, dovetailed case, in-stretcher, c1790 ($3,000-$3,500).

Reddish-brown Queen Anne mule chest, pine, lift-top chest that includes two real drawers and three false upper panels, cotter-pin hinges, c1750 ($3,500).

Decorated settee, grain and stencil-painted brown, mustard and red, original painted rush seat, c1810 ($3,500-$4,000).

Red bucket-bench, pine, great form, c1850 ($1,500).

ABC sampler, linen, signed "Margaret Dewitt," dated 1823 ($450).

Ship diarama, England, c1890 ($850).

Oil-on-canvas, Kentucky, young boy, by unknown primitive artist, late 19th century ($650).

Oval finger-lapped pantry boxes, painted surfaces, 19th century ($200-$375 each).

Bowl of stone fruit, late 19th century ($40-$150 each).

Game board, folding-book design, checkers (outside), backgammon (inside), paper shakers with bone dice, hand-turned chess pieces, c1890.

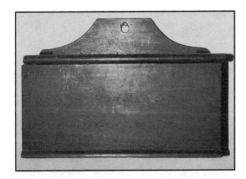

Hanging wall box, pine, original green paint, c1830 ($575).

Candlebox, pine, original red paint, slide-lip with hand-carved shell for pull, c1800 ($375).

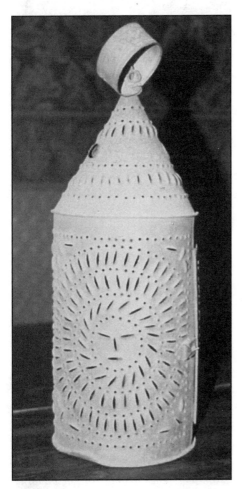

Early punched-tin lantern, rare face design, c1830 ($375-$450).

Wood and tin lantern, pine, original finish, c1850 ($475-$550).

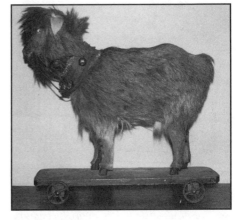

Goat pull toy, goat-fur body, c1880 ($850).

Hepplewhite mule chest, pine, lift-top chest with two drawers, original black-grained paint, c1800 ($3,500).

Set of counter drawers, walnut, square nails with old and unpainted finish, late 19th century ($425).

Early doll, Ludwig Greiner, leather body, 1858-72 ($575-$650).

Bucket bench, blue paint, half-moon ends, square-nail construction, mid 19th century ($450-$550).

Drop-leaf table, Southern origin, butterfly leaf with original brown paint, c1880 ($400-$450).

Tavern table, breadboard top, pegged construction, original red paint, c1850 ($900).

Painted cupboard from Missouri, combed-brown paint, pegged construction ($950-$1,250).

Stickspatter plates, late 19th century ($150).

Red-painted basket, unusual form ($200-$250).

Graphic hooked rug, 19th century ($250).

Pine dry-sink, salmon paint, 19th century ($1,800-$2,000).

Period Sheraton bench with original sage-green paint ($750).

Shaker swing-handled gathering basket in original black-green paint, mint condition, 19th century ($900-$1,200).

Pennsylvania painted dry-sink, rare form with drawers, c1870 ($3,500-$4,500).

Oil-on-board, New England, cows in pasture, artist unknown, c1890 ($475-$575).

Drop-handled pantry boxes, original putty and blue paint, c1870 ($450-$550 each).

Lone Star quilt, reds, mustard and shades of brown ($350-$400).

HRH ANTIQUES

Note: This section was prepared by Ron Hall of HRH Antiques in Clyde, N.C. Hall and his father operate an antiques shop at 394 Northwood Dr., Clyde, NC 28721, (704) 627-2342.

The past 12 months have seen an upswing in prices paid at auction. Traditional oak has joined walnut as the item most sought by newlyweds when they furnish their first home. On many a Saturday night, no matter the time of the year, there is sure to be a small auction or family porch sale to catch the interest of antiques collectors. It is in those Saturday night sit-down auctions that you can still find a treasure at a reasonable price. Antiques malls are now becoming one or two to every town, and, with many in the population looking for a steady job, selling the family-old dusty items is a new-found source of income.

This section was prepared using items that my family and I have been collecting for many years. Each member of my family has an area of special interest, and this has made the collecting task fun for all. My father, a very skilled furniture maker, has been trying to locate many of his family's early household pieces. My forefathers came into Western North Carolina from Scotland. They brought with them a genius for making what they needed. It is those particular items that are so highly sought by my generation. My mother loves the glass and china that was brought out for an "afternoon tea." My own interest has been the pottery of the Carolinas, since I live in an area in which much of it was made.

It is interesting to hear the stories about when the now-absent was commonplace. A case in point is a story my father tells about Pisgah Forest. When he was young, he would pass through there en route to work and see all the pottery out drying in the sun. Fine pieces were offered to him for $1 for choice.

My forefathers came into these mountains with a strong interest in making a better life. Everything they needed was here. The best woods—cherry, maple and walnut—were available in quantity. Large amounts of pine were also used. This is why so many great Southern furniture makers used as many as three or four woods in a piece of furniture.

B.B. Craig, swirl pottery jugs, 12", script signature ($4,500 each).

Seagrove Pottery dinner service by Dorthy Auman, service for four ($1,500).

Jugtown Pottery animals, attributed to Charles Moore ($300 each).

Moravian pottery from Old Salem—redware charger ($450); slip-decorated charger ($450).

From left: North Carolina pottery 6" drip-glaze vase by W.N. Owen ($250); 8" face jug by B.B. Craig ($300); 10" Cole Pottery Rebecca pitcher ($350).

Stickley wagon seat with mushroom turns, signed "Stickley, N.Y." on a side-stretcher, made of curly maple ($4,500).

Child's rocker horse from Tennessee ($600). The decoration on the base was alleged to be the view from the "great house" from which the horse originated.

Charleston, S.C., chest, pecan wood, inlay on top ($5,000).

Buncome County, N.C., cherry pie safe, original tins ($3,500).

Hitchcock child's highchair, original seat and stenciling ($850).

Curly-maple gate-leg table with three-board top, Sheraton turnings, c1810 ($1,500).

Eli Terry clock, wooden works, label inside back, great reverse painting ($7,500).

From left: Brace-back Windsor chair ($850); early curly-maple Chippendale chair with cattail seat ($1,000).

Mahogany snake-foot candlestand, water-wheel turnings ($750).

Wallace Nutting knuckle armchair, marked ($1,200).

From left: Two grain measures, each a half-bushel in size—measure with button-hole hoops ($250); measure with handles on the sides ($250).

Southern white-pine blanket chest with hidden storage drawer ($850).

From left: Marked B.B. Craig, chamber pot ($300); B.B. Craig bird house with mark ($350).

Cherry lowboy, original hardware, Virginia ($6,500).

East Tennessee lady's chest for storage, original hardware ($3,000).

Charleston flame-mahogany table ($750).

Yoke-back Windsor chair ($750).

Curly-maple flip-top candlestand ($750).

From left: LaBelle flow-blue 10" covered vegetable with fine brush work ($400); 8" pitcher ($600).

Martha Washington "hop skirt" rocking chair, early with original hickory bottom ($1,000).

Cast-iron kettle and a rare chestnut roaster that was considered a luxury in the mountains of North Carolina.

Early Eastern Tennessee baskets, rib construction, white oak ($250 each).

From left: The fry pan was brought to North Carolina from Kentucky ($175); maple dough board ($100); butter mold ($90); soapstone trivet ($75).

From left: Cedar piggin ($100); buttermilk pitcher ($175).

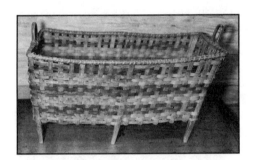

Early Cherokee baby basket ($500).

From left: Dough bowl ($250); butter paddles or "workers" ($75 each); flour scoop made from a can ($20).

From left: English Chintz porcelain, Royal Winton summertime pitcher ($350); summertime tray ($350); heather pitcher ($325).

From left: Flow-blue cheese with worm handle ($650); grape-pattern coffee with copper-luster detailing ($500); flower covered sugar ($450); butter-pat amoy ($45); wagon-wheel plate ($75).

From left: Fostoria American service, round cake plate ($100); square cake plate ($125); vinegar ($95); ashtray ($18); tall pitcher ($95); covered candy ($45); tumbler ($25).

Gaudy Welsh grape pattern #1, tea service ($1,850).

Gaudy Welsh urn pattern, luncheon set, part of service for eight ($4,000).

Flow-blue bowl and pitcher set by Johnson Brothers/England ($1,400).

Very old Christmas quilt, especially tiny stitching, c1890 ($1,000). This family heirloom was used only during the month of December.

From left: Roseville owl pitcher ($375); Roseville blackberry jardiniere ($375).

From left: Roycroft book ends with early mark ($135 for pair); Roycroft candle holder ($100).

Hand-made goose decoy from Ohio, great feathering with a red bill ($250).

Walnut game table from the Tidewater of Virginia, base is hand-shaped, hearts in each corner ($1,150).

Stagecoach mail trunk, leather, used from Syracuse, N.Y., to St. Joseph, Mo., 19th century ($950).

From left: Hand-whittled broom from North Carolina ($25); feather basket ($125).

Hall family flax wheel, chestnut and oak ($750).

COFFMAN'S COUNTRY ANTIQUES MARKET

Coffman's Country Antiques Market is located in Great Barrington, Mass., and offers the wares of more than 100 country and Americana dealers. The market contains 10,000 square feet of antiques merchandise and is open from 10 a.m. until 5 p.m. daily (except Easter, Christmas and Thanksgiving). You can reach Coffman's Country Antiques Market at Box 592, Jennifer House Commons, Rt. 7, Great Barrington, MA 01230.

Q&A with Joyce Coffman

Q. What is the biggest problem you face running a country antiques market?

A. Unquestionably, the biggest problem we have is trying to displace the preconceived idea that most serious collectors have about antiques malls. All of us have stopped and walked through aisles filled with 1950s furniture, crafts and record albums. Most of us have vowed never to return. Our business is not an antiques mall. We have 10,000 square feet of antique merchandise, with a regard for quality control and customer comfort.

Q. How do you make it attractive for customers to shop at your market?

A. Coming here to shop for Americana is like coming to a 100-dealer, quality-controlled antiques show that is open every day but Thanksgiving, Christmas and Easter. The merchandise is constantly changing, and the coffee is always on. We are also fortunate to have a knowledgeable and committed staff that can answer questions about the items for sale.

Q. What about pricing?

A. There is no commission paid on merchandise sold here, so the dealer doesn't have to build that into the selling price. If a customer possesses and can provide proof of a sales/resale tax number, that dealer will receive a "professional" discount of 10%. Prices aren't inflated, and that eliminates the need for any negotiations.

Q. For out-of-state customers, do you pack and ship?

A. We carefully package every item and can make arrangements for delivery or shipping, when necessary. We also provide a detailed and accurate sales receipt for everything.

Q. Do you have a mail-order business?

A. For mail customers, we have lists of items for sale with prices, descriptions and dimensions. Pictures are also available, and we send them throughout the United States. The categories of Americana that make up the lists include everything from decorated stoneware and dry sinks to Shaker and stone fruit. We offer the whole range of American country antiques.

Decorated yellow ware bowl ($125-$175).

Unusual spice storage box and individual spice boxes ($250-$350).

Toleware document box ($450-$550).

Yellow ware food mold, early 20th century ($115-$135).

Rockingham pottery spittoon ($300-$375).

Yellow ware rolling pin with maple handles ($100-$125).

Pair of French lanterns, brass ($375-$475 for pair).

Molded stoneware bowl, sponge decorated ($225-$325).

Glass mixer/beater ($250-$350).

Lantern with double match holders ($250-$375).

Blue-painted basket, early 20th century ($300-$350).

Black Americana stocking bottle doll with no face ($150-$200).

Birdseye-maple shaving mirror and box ($395-$495).

From left: Fishing creel with wooden lid ($250-$275); Pennsylvania rye-straw basket ($75-$125).

Tin mirrored candle sconce ($350-$400).

Miniature sewing machines ($225-$275 each).

Chalkware animals ($225-$295 each).

Chipped-carved tramp-art sewing box ($250-$375).

Banks, late 19th/early 20th century ($75-$150 each).

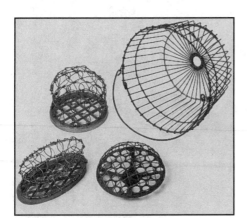
From left: Wire frogs ($35-$65 each); egg-gathering basket ($50-$65).

Salesman's sample washing machine and scrubbing board ($225).

Chocolate molds that produced rabbits for Easter ($95-$125 each).

Cake rack from a commercial bakery ($75-$200).

White oak-splint pack basket ($125-$150).

Copper tea kettle ($300-$450).

Game board, early 1900s ($125-$150).

Butter churn ($225-$450).

4-gallon "bird" crock, New York State, late 19th century ($200-$250).

Apple corer ($150-$250).

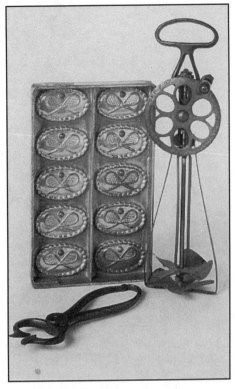

Ironstone tea pot ($175).

From left: Sugar nippers ($125-$150); early egg beater ($175-$200).

Wire parcel basket ($100-$200).

Graniteware teapot, early 20th century ($350-$400).

Splint basket with carved handles and a demi-john bottom ($125-$175).

Chipped-carved box lined with velvet ($250-$375).

Pair of cast-iron bookends, flowers in a basket ($275-$350).

COLLECTORS' CHOICE
ANTIQUE GALLERY

Collectors' Choice Antique Gallery of New Oxford, Pa., managed by Stan and Andrea Hollenbaugh, is generally considered to be one of the finest multi-dealer shops in the United States. With about 85 dealers, Collectors' Choice offers an exciting variety of country and period furniture and the best in accessories, including yellow ware, Pearlware, mocha, iron, toys, dolls, firearms and accouterments, sewing items, antique jewelry, textiles, ephemera, paintings and portraits. Collectors' Choice is open seven days a week and ships almost anything anywhere. The staff at Collectors' Choice has more than 100 years total experience in the antiques trade. Collectors' Choice may be reached at: 330 Golden Ln., New Oxford, PA 17350, (717) 624-3440. The gallery is open from 10 a.m. to 5 p.m. Monday through Saturday and noon to 5 p.m. on Sunday, or by special appointment.

Pair of Windsor Chairs with plaque, "Harvard 1782" ($5,800).

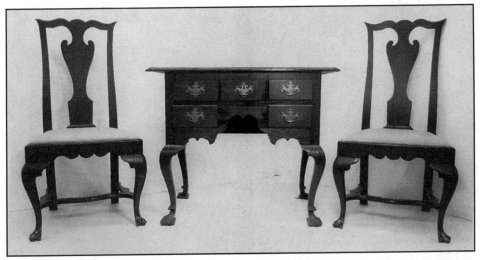

From left: Pair of Queen Anne Delaware Valley chairs ($7,800); Delaware Valley Queen Anne lowboy, some restoration ($15,900).

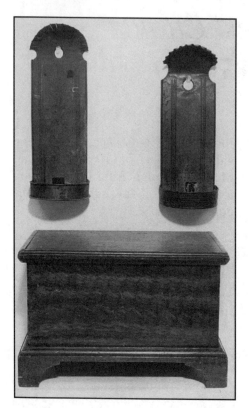

From top: Reverse-painted glass ($340); on wood ($395).

From left: Miniature decorated chest, York Co., Pennsylvania ($1,250); sconces ($295 each).

From left: Staffordshire Europa Platter, blue and white ($650).

From left: Three burl pieces ($725, $285, $475).

Multi-color lidded compotes, c1820 ($1,500 for pair).

From top: Pair of grain-painted miniature chests, York Co., Pennsylvania, 1830-50 ($995, $595).

From left: 7" Amberina pitcher, inverted thumbprint ($425); ivory and sterling corkscrew ($130); blue opalescent pitcher, inverted thumbprint ($200).

A blue and white York Co., Pennsylvania, quilt ($1,375).

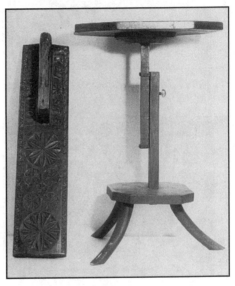

From left: Carved smoothing board, Scandinavian, dated 1705 ($895); Roger Bacon adjustable octagon-topped candlestand ($675).

From left: Pottery—Eberly flower pot, Strasburg, Va. ($950); 6-1/2" decorated stoneware pitcher ($1,100); 1-1/2 gallon stoneware crock, signed "B.C.M.," Milburn ($850).

From left: Silhouettes ($650, $545, $750).

New Geneva tanware ($1,250 each).

Fabulous decorated Lebanon Co., Pennsylvania, chest ($17,500).

Williamsport, Pa., sampler, 1830 ($1,475).

Wall cupboard, 32" wide, Monmouth Co., Virginia ($8,900).

From left: Sandwich glass—eight opalescent tie-backs ($1,000), candlestick ($490); candlestick, canary yellow ($580 for pair).

From left: 9" plate ($445); York Co., Pennsylvania, horn ($335); 10-3/4" plate ($825).

From left: Three Stiegel-type enamel bottles ($510, $390, $425).

From left: Three carved wooden nutcrackers ($125, $235, $215).

From left: Miniature painting on ivory ($700); hair necklace with 18k fittings ($965).

From top: Hand-painted tin toys ($400, $425, $825, $550, $350).

Iron hitching post, 28-1/2" ($525).

Chester Co., Pennsylvania, tilt-top candle-stand ($4,200).

From left: Iron teakettle ($365); tin eve scupper ($350); latch ($325).

Pair of portraits attributed to Vanderlyn, c1800 ($4,800).

Japanese tea service, attributed to "To-zan," five cups and saucers not shown ($2,450).

From left: Fabulous Schoenhut "Pony Blitz," all original ($16,000); glass-eye lamb ($775); glass-eye poodle ($900).

From left: Mocha—earthworm pitcher ($950); oyster pitcher ($1,400); large mug ($1,900).

Clockwise, from top: Decoys—Canada Goose by Madison Mitchell ($450); canvasback ($225); goldeneye, attributed Joe Lincoln ($475).

From left: Sandwich glass—Clambroth and blue candlestick ($590); whale-oil lamp, complete ($425); one of two canary candlesticks ($225 each).

"A Home in the Wilderness," Currier & Ives ($575).

From left: Rose Medallion/Rose Canton—lidded box ($975); covered vegetable ($685); sugar ($475).

"Lion in Love," by Frederick Stuart Church, 1833 ($295).

From left: Schoenhut—painted-eye giraffe, ($495); glass-eye polar bear ($1,250); painted-eye lion ($375).

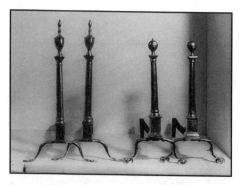

From left: Andirons—brass, penny feet, Newburgh, N.Y. ($1,800); claw and ball feet, plinth engraved with anchors and American eagle ($7,500).

From left: One of a pair of decorated New England Chippendale Chairs ($2,500); maple Queen Anne tea table, Massachusetts ($7,000).

186

From left: Signed Fulper bisque doll ($595); musical marotte ($795).

16" dome with hair flowers and doll ($1,200).

Harris and Schafer, Washington, D.C., sterling tea service ($6,000).

From left: Spatterware creamer and sugar ($2,200); creamer ($720).

From left: Pair of Delaware Valley Queen Anne side chairs ($7,900); Massachusetts William & Mary Desk ($7,500); mirror ($1,500).

Brown and light ochre-decorated Berks Co., Pennsylvania, blanket chest ($3,500).

From left: Ironstone ($150, $395, $275).

From left: Tramp art—($250, $425, $245).

From left: German Santa candy ($450); purple/pink spatter sugar ($500); Southwest Indian basket ($340).

From left: Painted wooden horse ($1,550); Cowden and Wilcox swan jug ($4,950).

From left: Redware—pitcher with brown, red and green glaze ($390); bowl with brown/cream rings ($490); mug with brown decoration ($440).

From left: Andirons—Massachusetts, brass ($1,475); Eastern Pennsylvania knife blade ($1,650); Philadelphia ($1,475).

From left: Staffordshire ($385); Duke and Duchess ($1,150 pair); spill vase ($650).

Cupboard, mustard and yellow ($1,125).

From left: Teakettle, signed "C. Kiefer" ($750); coin spoons, "John Myers, Phila." ($650); "Godbehere and Wiggin," sugar tongs ($135).

From left: Decoys—Mason mallards ($500 for pair); Jim Gurrier canvasback ($375); Henry Lockhard canvasback ($350).

From left: Dog ($365); stoneware with manganese decoration, Hagerstown, Md. ($850); painted Indian whirly-gig ($1,450).

From left: Blown glass—Baltimore Liberty and Union flask ($850); creamer ($195); decanter ($140); celery ($120).

From left: Lustre pitcher ($450); "Pelew" flow-blue compote ($750); lustre mug ($495).

From left: Steuben Aurene vase ($575); Peachblow vase ($295); Rookwood vase ($185).

Chippendale sponged-red corner cupboard ($6,400).

From left: Pair of milk-glass painted vases ($220); kerosene lamp ($168); milk-glass Santa ($145).

From left: Sheraton one-drawer stand, faux tiger maple ($1,150); yellow/brown stippled miniature chest ($575).

From left: Philadelphia low-back Windsor ($3,275); Queen Anne tea table ($2,800); New Jersey bannister-back ($2,900).

From left: 17-foot-long hooked runner ($875); hooked horse rug ($475); Chippendale slant-front desk, Massachusetts ($11,500).

Massachusetts highboy, some restoration ($16,500).

From left: Hepplewhite curly-maple gentlemen's chest ($5,250); Remmey crock ($975); decorated box ($885).

From left: Pearlware ($1,250, $295, $545).

From left: Decorated stoneware ($2,500, $7,500, $1,400).

Mahogany tall-clock, signed "William Cann" ($5,600).

From left: Chairs and tea table ($850, $595, $850).

From left: Free-blown colorless glass—sugar bowl ($835); berry bowl ($245); creamer ($170); chain decanter ($500).

From left: Sewing tables—American rose-wood/mahogany ($2,200); English ($1,250).

Cowden & Wilcox jug ($1,950).

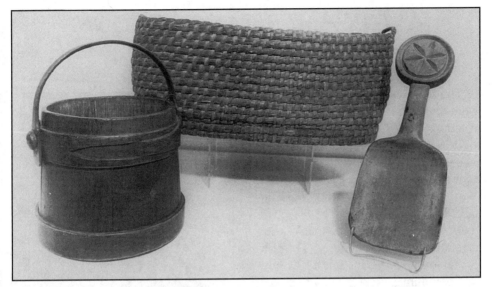

From left: Shaker bucket ($450); rye-straw basket ($725); butter scoop ($625).

From left: Mocha ($795); feather-edge compote ($395); Baltimore shaving mug ($395).

From left: Fan-back Windsor ($3,100); York Co., Pennsylvania, walnut farm table ($4,800); Frederick Co., Maryland, knuckle armchair ($3,950).

From left: Tramp Art ($725, $495).

ASTON AMERICANA AUCTIONS

The pictures and prices that follow were provided by Aston Americana Auctions (2825 Country Club Rd., Endwell, NY 13760-3349, 607-785-6598). The profusely illustrated Aston Americana catalogs have won awards from the New York State Auctioneers' Association. There is no charge to be placed on their mailing list for the annual spring and fall Americana auctions. (The prices that follow do not include a 10% buyer's premium.)

Pennsylvania step-back cupboard, two piece, exterior early over-painted, 42" long by 78" high, c1850 ($875).

From left: Tobacco cutter with iron horse blade ($160); hand-wrought iron rooster weathervane, top in original polychrome, c1840s ($1,100); folk iron rooster weathervane, top converted to a bootscraper ($140).

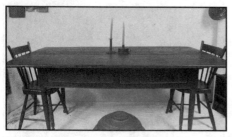

Center table in the Chippendale-style, Pennsylvania, 72" long by 39" wide by 29" high, c1800 ($1,350).

Pennsylvania wooden doughnut box, natural finish, 6" high by 12-1/2" diameter, c1860 ($100).

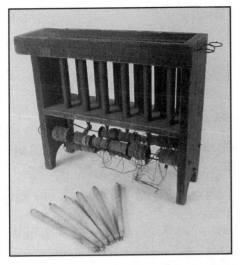

American candlemold, 18 pewter tubes with wick spools and rods intact, wooden case with bootjack feet, Nauvoo, Ill., c1840-50 ($1,650).

Highly carved walnut cookie roller, in style of Conger, deep floral imprint, 12" long, c1835 ($270).

From left: Victorian chalkware spaniel smoking a pipe, American, c1885 ($100); Gaudy Staffordshire plate, English, four-color floral design on cream, 9" diameter, c1830 ($70).

Victorian "horse pulled" baby carriage in original paint, metal rails and buggy wheels, English, molded composition horse covered with hand-stitched horse hide, real horse hair and mane, 58" long, c1875 ($2,300).

Butter print with rare lollipop handle, Pennsylvania, 6" long by 3" diameter, c1830 ($210).

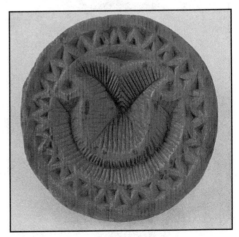

Butter print, Pennsylvania, deeply gouge-carved striated tulip design, encircled with border of chip and gouge-carved radiating triangles, 4" diameter, c1830 ($270).

Maltese cross "klappmodel" mold, five sections, 6-1/2" diameter, five sections with woman drawing water from pump, house with pine tree, tree in bloom, flowers, radiating tulips in center piece, c1880 ($420).

From left, clockwise: Four Pennsylvania butter prints ($80, $270, $220, $210).

Rare French tole-painted spiral candlestick with shade, mustard-yellow paint with floral design in black, 11" high, c1810 ($775).

Pair of carved wooden carnival knock-down figures, dressed with remnant of period clothing, American, late 19th century ($780 for pair).

From left: Three American baskets ($120, $190, $40).

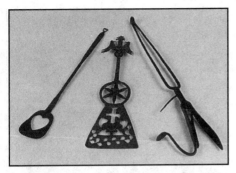

From left: Wrought-iron spatula, heart cut-out on blade, inlaid "TM 1774" on handle terminating in small, delicately cut heart for hanging, American, possibly Pennsylvania, 14-1/2" long ($575); wedding-gift spatula, iron with two distelfinks, incised rosettes, hearts and other decorations, 13" long ($550); pipe tongs, American, iron, nicely done, 18" long, 18th century ($625).

From left: Saffron cup attributed to Joseph Long Lehn, maple with lid, painted-strawberry design, pencil-signed inside "November 18, 1887," Lancaster Co., Pennsylvania, 6" high; five pieces of Peaseware—from left, behind saffron cup ($140, $110, $190, $380, $170).

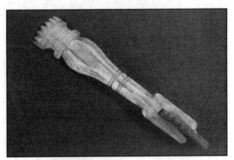

Class crown top, Lancaster Co., Pennsylvania, pie crimper, nicely carved bone with cookie cutter end, 5" long, c1820 ($300).

Early tavern cupboard, pine ($2,100).

Early Pennsylvania hanging cupboard ($700).

Gen. Santa Anna's belt of Battle of the Ala-
mo fame, c1830s-60s ($13,000).

Curly-maple chest of drawers, variably
sized bow-front drawers with milk-glass re-
sette pulls, tiger-maple pilasters ($1,850).

Half-column shelf clock, carved crest, sten-
ciled columns, Atkins & Downs, Bristol,
Conn., c1820 ($300).

Tall-case clock, eight-day moon phase,
probably Pennsylvania in origin, flame-
cherry case, freestanding pilasters and
flame finials ($5,600).

Close-up view of eight-day tall-case clock.

Close-up view of 30-hour tall-case clock

Tall-case clock, 30-hour, probably Pennsylvania origin, scroll-top bonnet, single finial, calendar aperture, linen-fold pilasters ($3,700).

Pilar-and-scroll shelf clock, "E. Terry & Son" (paper label), square dial, inset pilasters, c1820 ($1,600).

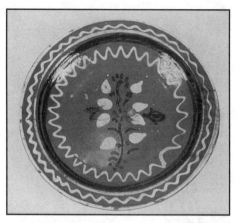

Slip-decorated shallow-form Moravian redware bowl, raised bottom, hairline and minor flaking, c19th century ($500).

Corner cupboard, two piece, flame cherry, probably Pennsylvania origin, 12 "light" over two paneled doors, straight bracket feet ($6,700).

Sgraffito and slip-decorated shallow-form bowl with hunting scene, yellow and green glaze, signed "Gleaves 1935" ($100).

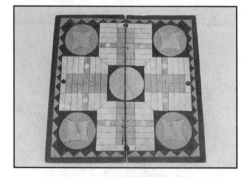

Early "pumper" firemen whirligig, early paint, replaced base and post ($375).

Pennsylvania German "Fik Muhl" five-color game board, signed "1901 John Ullrich, Lititz, Lancaster County" ($2,700).

Pennsylvania hutch table with unusual tapered legs, early grey-over-black paint, pegged, late 18th century ($1,400).

Rare folk-painted snake-joined lightning rod balls with spikes intact ($310).

Harry Folk-carved and applied doves and acorns slide lid "dues" box, probably Pennsylvania, c19th century ($850).

Sewing box, attributed to Joseph Long Lehn, decalcomania-style, dated 1875 ($875).

Folk-painted full-bodied whirligig, featuring "faceless" family of four ($2,900).

From left: Chip-carved double "lollipop" butter print with floral and relief carved crosshatch ($200); tape loom ($310).

Peaseware spice containers, footed, assembled set of eight in graduated sizes, one damaged finial ($1,800).

Elephant pull toy, carved from a single block of wood, some damage, 18th century ($860).

From left: Bride's box with painted figures of seated smoking man, woman and faint German script ($460); Bentwood ribbon box with freehand-painted tulips and floral designs, laced joining ($210); Bentwood trinket box with freehand-painted tulips and floral designs, laced joining ($300).

Circus wagon crest, highly carved eagle with lioness and dolphins, one lioness is missing ($650).

Civil War-era folk-carved pipe ($1,300).

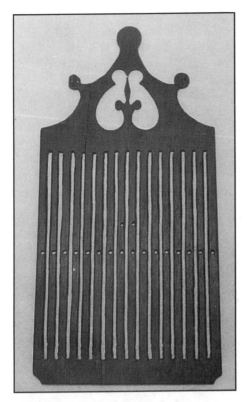

Redware tubed candlemold, 24 tubes with bootjack end-frame and fitted wooden cover, mid 19th century ($1,900).

Very early walnut tape loom with nicely cut-out decorative handle ($380).

From left: Black carnival knock-down figure, painted wooden lady in period clothing ($525); carnival knock-down figure of a man in period clothing ($450).

From left: Pictorial fraktur, watercolor-and-ink color design with rooster ($440); Pennsylvania scherenschnitte, scissor cutting, with watercolor-and-ink decorated pictorial featuring a distelfink and tulips ($1,250).

Redware bird whistle, modeled and wheel-thrown with clear lead glaze ($930).

Miniature highly carved Friesian-style box, slide top, signed "MWP 1779" ($875).

From left: Lamp fill can ($85); toddy warmer ($180); candle dipper ($260); doughnut box ($700); cheese press ($160); swizzle stick ($85).

From left: Nicely turned muffineer/sugar and cinnamon dispenser ($160); Peaseware spice container, bulbous-turned, small size with drop-handle ($250); nicely turned apothecary's double egg-cup measures ($160 for pair).

Delicately carved acorn-shaped nutmeg container with lid, American, 19th century ($100).

Little Bo Peep hooked rug ($30, a bargain).

From left: Concentrically turned spice grinder, probably Shaker, made "for the world" ($150); chip-carved double "lollipop" butter print with floral-and-relief carved crosshatch ($200).

Carved and painted pine oxen cart with original painted surface, all original with an excellent crazed surface, probably Pennsylvania in origin, 22" long by 5" high, early 20th century ($330).

Pennsylvania gouge-and-chip-carved bag stamp, "William Peter 1834" ($280).

Berks County hand-stitched and appliquéd stars-pattern quilt, 19th century ($800).

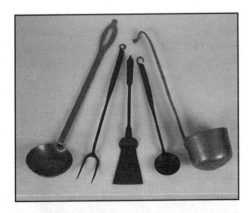

From left: Pennsylvania iron spoon, fork and spatula ($180); brass dipper and ladle ($48).

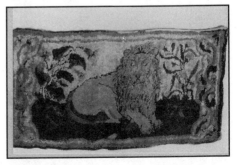

Polychromatic hooked lion rug, American, late 19th century ($440).

From left: 12-tube tin candlemold ($95); punched-tin lantern ($300); hogscraper with tin peg lamps ($70); 21-hole tin candlemold ($75).

From left: Hogscraper candleholder ($70); wooden noggin ($260); wooden plate ($85); knife and fork ($25).

From left: Redware charger ($210); pair of matched slip-decorated redware pie plates, good condition ($360); slip-decorated shallow-form Moravian redware bowl, raised bottom, hairline and minor flaking ($500).

From left: Pitcher, polychrome spongeware ($100); early splatter platter, central rose with leaves ($520); mug ($65); fish mold, Pearlware, late 18th century, probably English ($40).

"Lobster" quilt, c1840 ($1,100).

Folk-art moose table rug ($200).

"Loves First Kiss" folk-art box ($900).

Rare folk-art hooked rug depicting two standing bears playing with a red ball, superb original condition with extraordinarily strong colors, early 20th century, 43" by 29" ($1,200).

Pair of painted pine-twisted flame finials from Vermont, 12" high with a 5-1/2" diameter, attributed to Samuel McIntire or a carver of equal talent, late 18th/early 19th century ($675).

Carved Amish man and horse ($100).

Folk-carved Native American figure with painted tin headdress, Michigan Lakes origin, c1900 ($1,200).

Folk-art carved mortar and pestle ($250).

Rare Nantucket basket with lid ($650).

Rare goat butter print ($175).

Unusual table-top yarn swift with cup ($600).

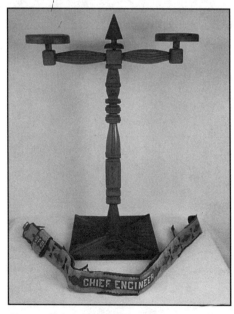

From left: Fireman's lantern holder ($725); chief engineer's leather belt ($110)

Burl mortar and pestle ($250).

From left: Pewter lighthouse coffeepot ($500); punched-tin coffee pot ($1,150).

Shenandoah redware creamer ($700).

From top: Civil War "camp" carved pipes ($500, $175).

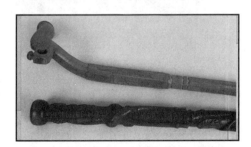

From left: Dean cane ($2,000); carved presentation cane ($300).

From left: Coin silver with swan finial ($200); coin-silver with fruit finial ($800).

12 "light" corner cupboard, c1840 ($1,700).

Spinning-wheel rocking chair ($95).

Pembroke table ($250).

From left: Berks County, Pennsylvania, hanging cupboard ($775); stoneware water cooler ($95); egg basket ($130); stoneware vendor's jug ($195); eel trap ($675).

From left: Folk-carved and painted "moon" face furniture crest with roosting bird top ($875); glazed redware mug, wheel-thrown with applied handle, mold chips on rim only ($45); glazed redware apple bank, nicely "polished" with paint decorations ($390).

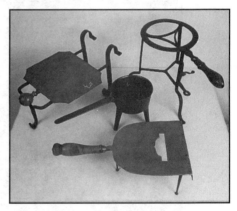

Classic "strutting cockerel" weathervane ($540).

"Fragment" blanket chest end-board with painted tulip design ($75).

From left: Trivet with brass plate ($225); tiger-maple handle trivet with brass plate ($275).

18th century tiger-maple tavern table ($650).

Bracket-base blue blanket chest ($425).

COPAKE COUNTRY AUCTIONS

Michael Fallon is an auctioneer and appraiser who conducts regularly scheduled cataloged Americana auction sales of formal and country furniture, Shaker items, quilts, coverlets, hooked rugs, samplers and folk art. Each year, the Copake Country Auction also conducts the "best bicycle sale in the world," featuring antique bicycles and related memorabilia. Fallon is a member of numerous state and national associations for auctioneers. The items that follow have been sold recently at Copake Country Auctions. Fallon can be contacted at Copake Country Auctions, Box H, Copake, NY 12516, (518) 329-1142, fax (518) 329-3369. The Copake Country Auction is located in Columbia County off Route 22, with easy access from the Taconic State Parkway.

Large folio, period, Currier and Ives ($935).

Early library book, Dictionaire De Marine #16 ($1,100).

Water color, folk painting of Teddy Roosevelt at a Maine camp ($4,400).

"Kit" quilt, Pennsylvania, c1930 ($740).

19th century Pennsylvania star quilt ($600).

Pennsylvania sampler quilt, c1885 ($5,500).

Duchess County, New York, coverlet, 1838 ($990).

Close-up view of Duchess County, New York, coverlet.

Needlepoint Bessarabian rug, Helen Hayes estate ($2,970).

19th century English tea table ($3,850).

Grenfell knitting bag ($715).

19th century Quaker sampler ($1,100).

Round oak table with claw feet ($935).

Close-up view of round oak table with claw feet.

19th century Zoar, Ohio, bed ($660).

18th century fan-carved Queen Anne high-boy ($8,250).

Vermont decorated blanket chest, c1820 ($1,265).

From left: Miniature chest, c1820 ($1,375); 19th century figural andirons ($440); child's box, c1800 ($990).

19th century decorated blanket box, New York State, one drawer, from Albany County ($1,430).

Tiger-maple Queen Anne tall-chest ($5,700).

19th century French Canadian kas ($2,750).

18th century Pennsylvania Chippendale secretary, "marriage" of top and bottom sections ($3,400).

18th century Pennsylvania dower chest, "as found" ($2,860).

18th century Pennsylvania hanging corner cupboard ($4,675).

Card table with rare original oil-cloth cover, c1810 ($4,675).

Pie safe, unusually detailed tins, 19th century ($1,540).

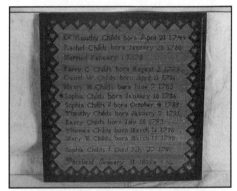

Detailed family record, 1805 sampler ($880).

Early English "coaching" table, c1690-1710 ($2,400).

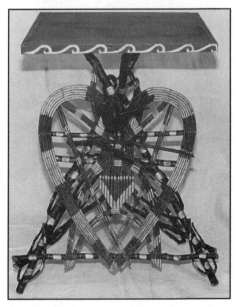

Folky Adirondack twig stand ($880).

Northshore sofa, c1815 ($7,150).

19th century Sheraton server with four chairs, all in original paint ($1,650 for set).

Shaped-top Chippendale serving table, New England, c1800 ($825); schoolmaster's desk from Maine, c1810 ($1,210).

L. & J.G. Stickley bookcase ($4,620).

Eastern Pennsylvania, dower chest, "as found," c1770 ($7,040).

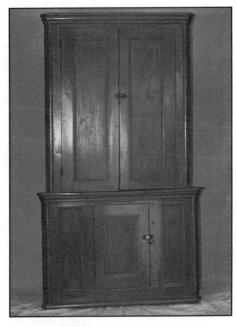

Canadian corner cupboard, c1840 ($1,430).

Two-part refinished Dutch cupboard, 19th century ($4,400).

12-foot harvest table, New York State, original surface, 19th century ($2,970).

Excellent condition, Coca-Cola advertising, c1937 ($990).

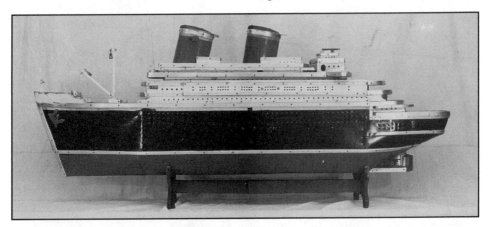

Unusually large ship model, folk art, 90" in length ($715).

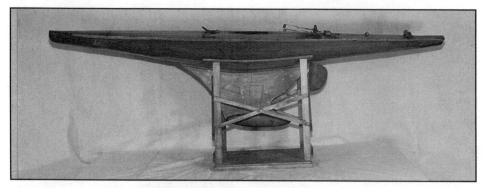

Early 20th century pond boat, original condition ($990).

Two-drawer tiger-maple stand, c1815 ($990).

Folky boat model or child's toy, early 1900s, original painted surface ($300).

From left: Iron kettle, signed "Wm. Tilson" ($605); New York State "bird" decorated batter jug ($220).

From left: Spanish-foot Queen Anne side chair, c1790 ($715); Queen Ann serpentine-top tea table, 18th century ($2,500).

Close-up view of Somerset stoneware water cooler.

Somerset stoneware water cooler, incised decoration and cobalt ($2,035).

Minton bowl with underplate ($2,970).

Running-horse weathervane ($1,320).

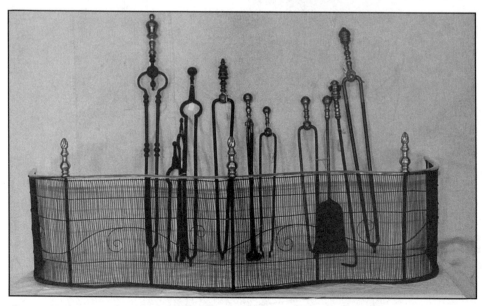

Serpentine wire-screen fender ($5,500).

19th century Pennsylvania gilt eagle ($3,520).

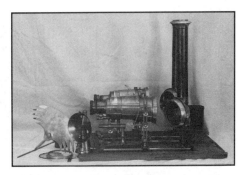

Rare 19th century French parablon ($1,050).

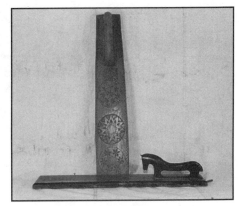

Two 19th century manger boards ($745 each).

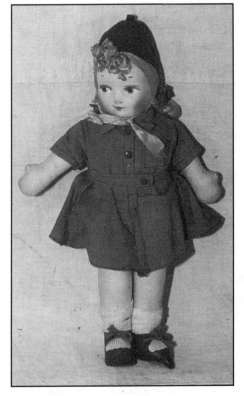

Rare Girl Scout doll ($75).

From left: Two period mirrors ($1,200, $685).

Cast-iron fireplace set ($990).

From left: Fighting cock weathervane ($1,760); Ethan Allen horse weathervane ($525).

JOY LUKE AUCTION GALLERY

The Joy Luke Auction Gallery is an auction and appraisal company that conducts estate and consignment cataloged auctions and specialized sales throughout the year, featuring estate jewelry, Indian artifacts, dolls, toys, textiles, Americana, advertising and furniture. The Joy Luke auctioneers are members of the National Auctioneers Association and the Illinois State Auctioneers Association. Auctions are advertised nationally, regionally and locally and attract buyers from across the United States and numerous countries around the world. The auctions are conducted in a well-appointed gallery with comfortable seating for 300 bidders. Contact Joy Luke Auction Gallery at 300 E. Grove St., Bloomington, IL 61701, (309) 828-5533, fax (309) 829-2266.

20th century oak china cabinet with glass door, curved-glass side panels, glass shelves, carved top with oval mirror, 77" high ($200).

Walnut postmaster's desk with drop-front, two drawers, 52" high, 30" wide, desk came from the Kangley, Ill., Post Office that closed in 1925 ($300).

From left: Mixed-wood diminutive china cabinet with two glass doors and cupboard at base, 41" high by 20" wide ($100); pine-hooded rocking baby cradle ($70).

Elaborate Victorian renaissance walnut-and-burl sideboard, beveled mirror, four ornately carved candle shelves, white marble top, paneled sides, 109" high by 74" deep ($6,050).

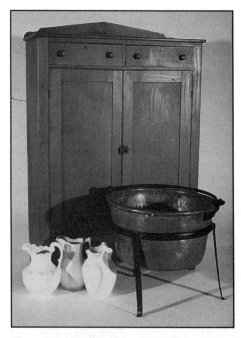

Victorian cherry secretary/china cabinet with drop-front desk, one drawer, 67" high by 37-1/2" wide ($300).

From left: Walnut jelly cupboard with two half-drawers at top, two cupboard doors and full drawer at base, 64" high by 44" wide by 18" deep ($475); large copper candle-kettle with iron bail-handle and iron stand ($125).

Pine cabinet with glass door, four shelves and lower cupboard, 78-1/2" high by 41" wide ($350).

Victorian walnut and birdseye-maple fall-front desk with carved top rail and shelf, fall-front writing surface and one full drawer, 62-1/2" high by 29-1/2" wide ($450).

From left: Early platform rocking armchair ($125); primitive pine bin with slant-front lid, 27-1/2" high by 29" wide ($190).

From left: Pine jelly cupboard with two half-drawers at top, two wooden doors, 51" high by 46" wide ($400); pine dry sink with lower cupboard, 25" high by 32" wide ($120).

Oak china cabinet with three glass-paneled doors and three lower drawers, 63" high by 63" wide ($550).

Walnut pie safe with 12 pierced-tin side panels, 51" high by 41" wide ($350).

Oak commode with upper towel bar, two lower doors and one drawer ($175).

Victorian walnut armoire with two doors and two lower half-drawers, 96" high by 56" wide ($375).

Early 18th century English oak chest of drawers with two half-drawers, two full drawers, original brass tear-drop pulls, bracket feet, top board cracked, 31" high by 31" wide ($1,100).

Early English Mahogany writing desk with two adjustable book stands, writing desk with drawer for pens, two pull-out candle shelves and adjustable stand ($550).

19th century American mahogany corner armchair ($132).

Oak china cabinet with framed beveled-glass mirror, two glass doors, glass side panels and two drawers at base, 75" high by 50" wide ($1,750).

Oak post office letter holder with brass mounted plate, from Kangley, Ill., Post Office that closed in 1925, 41" high by 73" long ($600).

Victorian walnut-and-burl high-back youth bed with carved head on crest, 64" high by 59" long by 40" wide ($550).

Bentwood baby cradle ($70).

Early primitive pine kitchen cupboard with lower door, three upper shelves, 76-1/2" high by 37-1/2" wide by 13" deep ($450).

Marx tin toy, "Medieval Castle Fort" with knights, soldiers and horses, in original box ($120).

Carved oak high-back bench, 42-1/2" high by 48" wide ($250).

Mission oak desk with one drawer and two side book shelves, 30" high by 48" long ($175).

Louis XV-style lady's writing desk with painted decoration 51" high by 37" wide ($1,200).

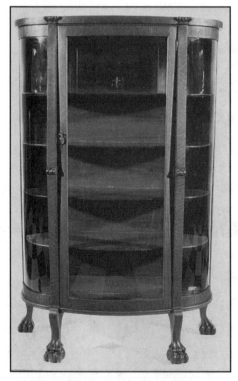

Oak carved-glass china cabinet with four shelves, 60-1/2" tall by 39" wide ($750).

Eastlake Victorian walnut-and-burl parlor table with brown and white marble top, ornate carved base, 29" high by 29-1/2" wide ($300).

Ornate Victorian walnut-and-burl bed-room set, purchased in 1881, high-back bed with footboard and side rail, dresser, wash-stand, all original ($3,900).

Ornately carved walnut sideboard/cup-board with carved crest, bun feet, 98" high by 60" wide ($1,300).

English 19th century rosewood round tilt-top dining table with pedestal base, carved feet, 52" diameter ($1,700).

English walnut high-back sideboard with ornately carved mirrored back, 95" high by 60" wide ($1,600).

Victorian walnut pump organ, 78" high by 48" wide and organ stool with metal claw and glass-ball feet, adapted to use an electrically operated motor for the bellows ($225).

Mahogany secretary/bookcase with two glass doors, slant-front desk, three full drawers, 78-1/2" high by 37" wide ($850).

Maple dresser, four mahogany veneer-fronted full drawers and two half-drawers, 50" high by 45-1/2" wide, c1850 ($240).

Walnut chest of drawers with two stepback half-drawers and four full drawers, 48" high, 44" wide by 48" high.

Mission oak library table with one drawer and lower shelf, original copper hardware, 29-1/2" high ($550).

Walnut bookkeeper's desk with two upper cupboards, slant-front, lift-top writing desk, 64" high by 48-1/2" wide ($600).

Walnut jelly cupboard with two upper half-drawers, two glass doors and two shelves, 61" high ($450).

Late 18th century English country wavyline ladder-back dining armchair with woven rush seat ($385).

English walnut case school-house clock with fusee movement, time only, 11-1/2" diameter ($225).

Molded redware pottery pitcher with high-relief figures, "The Gypsies," 7-1/4" high ($88).

Wedgwood blue-and-white pottery teapot "The Wesley Teapot," damaged at spout and hairline crack ($60).

Hull Pottery tea set, teapot "B 20-6," sugar "B 22-4," creamer "B 21-4" ($350).

Green and white parian pitcher with molded high-relief figures, two men drinking, seated man smoking, man and woman dancing, 9" high ($165).

Walnut-case shelf clock with Eastlake decoration, glass-panel door decorated with Niagara Falls, marked "Niagara," time, strike and alarm movement ($150).

Ansonia oak-case wall clock with time and strike, 37" high ($400).

Framed oil-on-canvas, grazing Highland cattle, signed lower right "W. Watson 1902," marked on verso, "By Highland Stream-Glen Crowe, Argyleshire, Wm. Watson," 29" by 44" ($5,500).

Gilbert oak-case cabinet clock, decorated with carved deer, dogs and hunting scene, ornate metal dial, time and strike, 14" high ($150).

19th century oval-framed oil-on-canvas, genre scene, signed lower left "William Will," ornate gilded frame, verso of canvas marked "Prepared by Charles Roberson, 51 Long Acre, London CR1546," canvas 25" by 30", overall 32" by 38" ($5,500).

Toy cap-gun, marked "Cowboy" with steer head on handle ($70).

Ithaca walnut-case No. 4 hanging office calendar wall clock with single door, double dial, day, date and month, time and strike, 29" high ($875).

French black-marble mantel clock with six columns, metal and porcelain dial marked "Kemp Bros. Union St. Bristol," beveled-glass crystal, time and strike ($225).

Framed oil-on-board, portrait of young slave girl, "Nellie Fostina Esiava," signed lower left "A.M. Hiatt," 7" by 7" ($250).

Rare painted wooden school house, complete with four student desks with 12 girl dolls, teacher's desk and chair and typical contents of school of the period, hinged lift-up top and removable front wall, 21" high by 27" long by 17" deep ($1,100).

From left: Russian-spun cotton Santa with papier-mâché lace, 13" high ($160); Russian cotton and papier-mâché Santa figurine, 15" high ($90); Russian Santa figure with blue fabric coat and gold trim, 24-1/2" tall ($325).

Marx painted-tin toy circus "The Big Top," with two billboards and large collection of rubber and plastic animals and circus figures ($140).

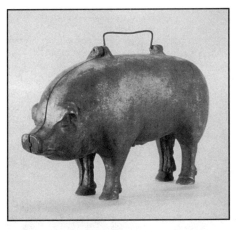

Iron Aunt Jemima Penny Bank, paint chipped, and plastic Uncle Moses salt shaker ($40 for pair).

Rare cast-iron model of standing pig box with handle, hinged down the center, opens to reveal skeleton and internal organs of the pig with cylindrical wells, marked "Property of Moorman Mfg. Co. Quincy, Ill.," 15-1/2" long by 9" high ($1,400).

Pine baby buggy with metal frame, green upholstery, excellent refinished condition ($225).

Marx tin toy wind-up motorcycle and rider ($280).

J. Chein & Company mechanical tin Ferris Wheel with six cars and bells, mint condition, original box ($375).

Old Sleepy Eye pottery salt jar decorated with bust of Indian, 6-1/4" diameter, chip at base ($500).

From left: Heubach bisque-head character baby doll, painted eyes, open mouth, composition body, 20" high ($700); bisque character baby doll, marked "K (Star) R", painted eyes, open mouth, composition body, 18" high ($675); bisque character baby doll, marked "C/3," blue sleep eyes, open mouth, 16-1/2" high ($150).

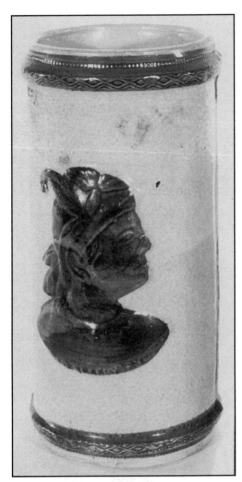

Oak shop display case for "Merrick's Six Cord Soft Finish Spool Cotton," curved-glass side panels, mirrored sides, one glass panel broken, 23-1/2" high by 32" across ($800).

Old Sleepy Eye pottery cylindrical vase, decorated with bust of Indian, 8-3/4" high ($350).

Large mounted water buffalo head trophy, 38" deep by 40" across ($1,045).

18th century English silver gilt-lidded pedestal urn with repousse grapes and leaves, 25-1/2" high, urn hallmarked London 1766, base hallmarked London 1839 and 1898 ($3,410).

Bisque white hen on basketweave nest, 7" high by 8-1/4" long ($360).

Pair of matching cobalt-sblue glass oil lamps ($110 for pair).

Walnut secretary/bookcase, two glass doors, fall-front writing surface, three full drawers, 85" high by 42-1/2" wide ($700).

Set of four 18th century Dutch Colonial marquetry side chairs, all-over floral inlay decoration, needlepoint and petite point upholstered seats ($1,760 for set of four).

CHAPTER 9
THE TEST

Final Examination #15

Serious alterations in the American education system have forced us to reconsider the manner in which this test is constructed, administered and scored. Historically, we have used as a norm group for statistical comparisons, a gathering of used-car salesmen that meets daily at a coffee shop/religious snake store in Findlay, Il.

These gentlemen represent a cross-section of Americana that statistically meets our needs and budget. Several would have served with the military (American) during the Vietnam-era but were vacationing in Canada when the draft notices appeared in their mail boxes. By the time they returned to the United States, the war had ended, and they were able to get on with their careers.

The majority have a high-school education, with 63.8% also having achieved some post-graduate work at institutions varying from Buster's Home for Hair to Pistol Bob's Welding College. Three have an extensive background in the complex world of auctions at Harriet's Bicycle and Auto Auction Haus in Hazel, Tenn. As a group, their collecting interests include left-footed G.I. Joe boots, insects, used car-related memorabilia, hair nets, Shaker, canning jar rubbers, orange-crate labels and 19th century painted furniture.

The simple fact of a change in the internal makeup of the norming group has altered forever the manner in which this final examination is put together. Keep in mind that in America, a man or group of men is considered innocent until proven guilty, and these charges would never have been brought in Mississippi or Montana. Applications are now being accepted at Buster's Home of Hair for the 16th edition of this book.

(The answers to the examination are at the end of this section.)

1. **This stoneware crock dates from about:**
   a. Could be after 1900
   b. Probably before 1860
   c. Anytime from 1830-1900

2. **True or False**
   It gives every indication as being produced in New York or Pennsylvania.

3. **A crock like this example in pristine condition is worth about:**
   a. $35
   b. Less than $100, but more than $35
   c. More than $113

4. **True or False**
   This cupboard appears to be made of oak and dates from about 1840.

5. **True or False**
   If this cupboard was painted blue rather than green, its value would be increased by a minimum of 25%.

6. **True or False**
   If the glass in all 12 panes has been replaced, the value of the cupboard would decrease by a minimum of 25%.

7. **True or False**
   This cupboard is worth a minimum of $3,500.

9. True or False

This chair has a splint seat.

10. True or False

This chair is probably made from more than one type of wood.

11. True or False

This chair could date as early as 1820.

12. This chair contains:

  a. Finials, stretchers, ladder-back, splint seat

  b. Rush seat, finials, stretchers

  c. Turned legs, sack-back, finials

13. True or False

In chrome-yellow paint, this cupboard is worth a minimum of $1,650.

14. True or False

This cupboard would date prior to 1800.

15. The least valuable candlemold is:
a. The one on the left
b. The example in the middle
c. The mold on the right

16. These Candlemolds are:
a. Products of the 18th century
b. More often found made of redware than tin
c. Neither of the above are correct.

17. True or False
A check for $623.31 would *not* buy these three candlemolds.

18. Shaker boxes
a. Usually are made of oak and poplar
b. Usually are made of pine
c. Usually have maple sides and a pine top

19. True or False
The Shakers were thriving in New England by 1700, and all but gone by 1900.

20. True or False
A check for $1,000 would buy these five boxes.

21. Which state did not have a Shaker community?
a. Indiana
b. Kentucky
c. Illinois
d. Ohio

22. Most of the Shaker production rocking chairs were made in:
a. Canterbury, N.H.
b. Mt. Lebanon, N.Y.
c. Lebanon, Pa.
d. Pleasant Hill, Ky.

23. This hobo was made in:
 a. Pennsylvania
 b. Germany
 c. Austria
 d. None of the above

24. The hobo dates from about:
 a. Early 1900s
 b. 1920s/early 1930s
 d. 1940s
 d. Late 1930s/early 1940s

25. True or False
 The hobo was made by the Schoenhut Company and is more than $200.

26. True or False
 The 4-gallon jug dates after 1890.

27. True or False
 The cobalt bird was put onto the surface of the jug with a brush.

28. True or False
 This jug is worth a minimum of $850.

29. True or False

The basket dates from the first half of the 19th century.

30. True or False

It could be described as a handcrafted splint basket with a single-wrapped rim.

31. True or False

This chest dates from the first half of the 19th century.

32. True or False

Refinished, it is worth about $125-$150.

33. True or False

In blue paint, it is worth more than $295.

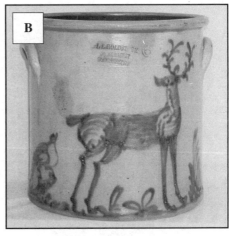

Questions 31-35 are concerned with American stoneware. Use the four examples (a, b, c, d) to answer the questions.

34. The most valuable piece of stoneware is ___

35. The two pieces that are slip-decorated are ___ and ___

36. The piece covered with Albany slip is ___

37. The ovoid pieces are ___

38. Of the four examples, the last piece made was ___

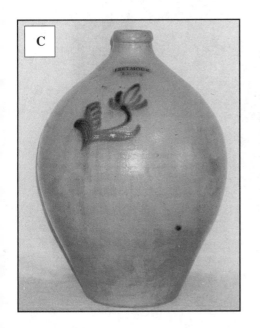

39. True or False

This soda case is worth about $15-$25.

40. This picnic basket:
    a. Is rare and I love it.
    b. Is not rare, and I am indifferent to-
      ward it.
    c. Will change my life forever if I buy
      it.

41. The basket dates from about
    a. Yesterday
    b. Thursday
    c. Baskets of this vintage are difficult
      to date because the same styles were
      made over a long period of time.

(Questions 42-45: Match the last name to the event or area of expertise with which it is associated.)

___ 42. York, Pa., antiques shows   a. Hayward

___ 43. Museum of American Folk Art   b. Gould

___ 44. Early American wooden ware   c. Burk

___ 45. Early lighting   d. Bishop

Essay Question (5 points, choose either question)

1. Describe in detail the chronological and historical development of the North American red radish industry from the 1860s through 1954. This was discussed in detail in class on Feb. 13 (Tuesday). If you were not in class and missed the information, you will now pay the piper.

2. Discuss the significance of the landmark auction of' the Tab Hunter Collection of Americana at Harold's Motel in Bayonne, N.J., in 1989, and its lasting impact on the prices collectors must deal with in today's market.

Correct Responses

1. a	13. True	25. True	37. a,c,d
2. False	14. False	26. False	38. b
3. b	15. b	27. False	39. True
4. False	16. c	28. True	(maybe less)
5. True	17. True	29. False	40. b
6. False	18. c	30. False	41. c
7. True	19. False	31. False	42. c
8. False	20. False	32. True	43. d
9. False (rush)	21. c	33. True	44. b
10. True	22. b	34. b	45. a
11. True	23. a	35. b,c	
12. b	24. b	36. d	

Scoring Scale

46-50 correct responses

A unique opportunity awaits you in the world of retail. Your score indicates potential employment at your local Wal-Mart in the interior-design department. Wal-Mart may want to start you as a greeter because of your sparkling personality.

41-45 correct responses

Certainly an above average score, employment possibilities at a local paint store, massage parlor or shoe-repair shop. Watch Psychic Friends Network for further updates.

36-40 correct responses

Probably not representative of your talents; score indicates potential for work in heavy construction, sandwich-making or nuclear research.

35 or less correct responses

It would probably be advantageous to pursue other interests than Americana. If you persist, it could become unpleasant and complicated.

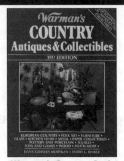
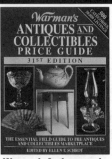